MULTIPLICATION WORKBOOK

FOR DIGITS 0 - 12

AGES 7+

PRACTICE 100 DAYS OF MATH DRILLS

with

RONNY the FRENCHIE

TABLE OF CONTENTS

Answer Keys Included at the Back

INTRODUCTION

Hi kids!

It's your favorite French Bulldog Ronny, back again and excited to go on a learning journey all about multiplication. If you haven't met me before, the most important thing to know is that I love knowledge (almost as much as I love bananas)! I got struck by lightning on top of the Eiffel Tower and my brain grew bigger, as well as my appetite for knowledge. Now I'm a fact-sniffing, globe-trotting, banana-loving French bulldog and I want you to join me!

In this book, we're going to be learning about multiplication. When I first heard about multiplication, I was very confused, so I had to look it up in my trusty dictionary.

An easier way to put it is:

To multiply something means to add the same number to itself a certain amount of times.

So, if I had 2 bananas and I multiplied them by 3, I would add my 2 bananas together 3 times.

2 + 2 + 2 = 6 delicious bananas!

Along the way, I'll be cheering you on (and maybe keeping you awake!) with some super interesting and exciting facts all about math. These are facts that I've gathered from all over the world and include rivetingly recent facts as well as amazingly ancient ones too! There is so much knowledge to cover, I just know you'll have a great time learning about multiplication. My little bull-dog tail is wagging with excitement! Don't worry if you don't get it straight away. With me by your side, we'll have you answering questions faster than a calculator in no time!

DAY 1
· Multiplying 0 & 1 ·

1) 1 × 8

2) 3 × 1

3) 1 × 9

4) 8 × 1

5) 0 × 7

6) 3 × 1

7) 0 × 4

8) 1 × 1

9) 0 × 7

10) 8 × 0

11) 0 × 4

12) 2 × 1

13) 0 × 7

14) 5 × 1

15) 0 × 7

16) 7 × 0

17) 1 × 4

18) 2 × 0

19) 0 × 4

20) 2 × 1

21) 1 × 5

22) 7 × 1

23) 0 × 3

24) 9 × 1

25) 0 × 9

26) 5 × 1

27) 1 × 6

28) 1 × 1

29) 1 × 8

30) 5 × 0

31) 1 × 8

32) 6 × 1

33) 1 × 3

34) 1 × 0

35) 0 × 7

36) 9 × 0

37) 1 × 2

38) 1 × 1

39) 0 × 3

40) 6 × 0

41) 0 × 6

42) 8 × 0

43) 0 × 4

44) 1 × 1

45) 1 × 5

46) 3 × 1

47) 1 × 5

48) 3 × 1

49) 1 × 9

50) 6 × 1

51) 0 × 9

52) 1 × 1

53) 1 × 7

54) 1 × 0

55) 0 × 6

56) 5 × 0

57) 0 × 1

58) 2 × 1

59) 0 × 3

60) 4 × 1

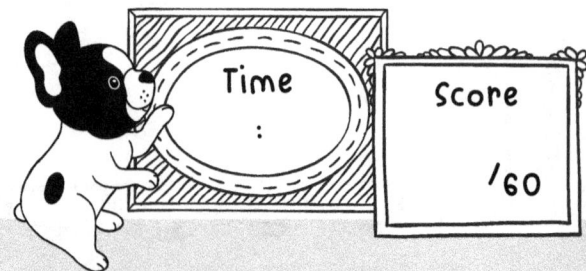

Time :

Score

/60

DAY 2
· Multiplying 0 & 1 ·

1)   0
  × 9

2)   7
  × 1

3)   0
  × 9

4)   7
  × 0

5)   0
  × 1

6)   9
  × 0

7)   1
  × 7

8)   2
  × 1

9)   1
  × 10

10)   9
  × 0

11)   0
  × 11

12)   4
  × 0

13)   1
  × 10

14)   9
  × 1

15)   1
  × 9

16)   12
  × 0

17)   1
  × 8

18)   7
  × 1

19)   1
  × 10

20)   8
  × 0

21)   1
  × 10

22)   8
  × 0

23)   0
  × 10

24)   6
  × 1

25)   0
  × 5

26)   1
  × 1

27)   0
  × 10

28)   12
  × 1

29)   0
  × 5

30)   1
  × 1

31)   1
  × 3

32)   4
  × 1

33)   0
  × 7

34)   8
  × 0

35)   1
  × 5

36)   12
  × 0

37)   1
  × 1

38)   9
  × 1

39)   0
  × 2

40)   10
  × 0

41)   1
  × 1

42)   2
  × 1

43)   0
  × 8

44)   2
  × 1

45)   1
  × 8

46)   7
  × 0

47)   1
  × 12

48)   6
  × 1

49)   0
  × 8

50)   3
  × 1

51)   1
  × 8

52)   3
  × 0

53)   0
  × 7

54)   9
  × 0

55)   0
  × 8

56)   11
  × 0

57)   1
  × 1

58)   4
  × 0

59)   0
  × 6

60)   1
  × 0

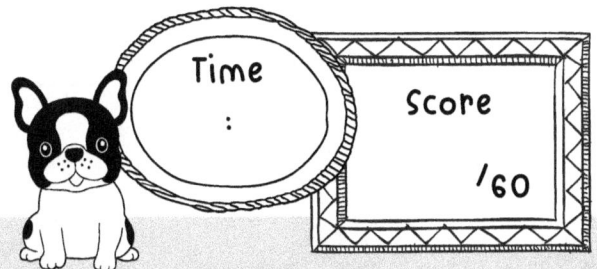

Time
:

Score

/60

DAY 3
· Multiplying 0 & 1 ·

1)   1 × 8
2)   9 × 0
3)   0 × 1
4)   3 × 1
5)   0 × 12
6)   10 × 1
7)   0 × 6

8)   1 × 0
9)   1 × 6
10)   3 × 1
11)   0 × 8
12)   11 × 1
13)   1 × 8
14)   10 × 1

15)   1 × 2
16)   12 × 1
17)   1 × 12
18)   12 × 0
19)   1 × 3
20)   12 × 1
21)   0 × 3

22)   4 × 0
23)   0 × 8
24)   5 × 0
25)   0 × 8
26)   5 × 1
27)   1 × 11
28)   5 × 1

29)   1 × 1
30)   12 × 0
31)   0 × 5
32)   7 × 0
33)   1 × 3
34)   6 × 1
35)   0 × 8

36)   8 × 0
37)   0 × 6
38)   8 × 0
39)   1 × 12
40)   3 × 0
41)   1 × 1
42)   6 × 0

43)   1 × 8
44)   4 × 0
45)   0 × 7
46)   5 × 1
47)   0 × 8
48)   7 × 0
49)   1 × 12

50)   2 × 0
51)   0 × 11
52)   11 × 0
53)   1 × 1
54)   2 × 0
55)   0 × 6
56)   9 × 1

57)   0 × 11
58)   6 × 1
59)   1 × 9
60)   2 × 1

Time :

Score /60

DAY 4
· Multiplying 2 ·

1) 2
  × 5

2) 6
  × 2

3) 2
  × 3

4) 3
  × 2

5) 2
  × 3

6) 6
  × 2

7) 2
  × 9

8) 4
  × 2

9) 2
  × 2

10) 6
   × 2

11) 2
   × 8

12) 2
   × 2

13) 2
   × 9

14) 5
   × 2

15) 2
   × 2

16) 7
   × 2

17) 2
   × 7

18) 6
   × 2

19) 2
   × 2

20) 7
   × 2

21) 2
   × 3

22) 4
   × 2

23) 2
   × 8

24) 5
   × 2

25) 2
   × 8

26) 6
   × 2

27) 2
   × 5

28) 6
   × 2

29) 2
   × 7

30) 7
   × 2

31) 2
   × 3

32) 5
   × 2

33) 2
   × 6

34) 2
   × 2

35) 2
   × 3

36) 5
   × 2

37) 2
   × 9

38) 9
   × 2

39) 2
   × 4

40) 6
   × 2

41) 2
   × 9

42) 6
   × 2

43) 2
   × 5

44) 2
   × 2

45) 2
   × 4

46) 4
   × 2

47) 2
   × 4

48) 4
   × 2

49) 2
   × 7

50) 5
   × 2

51) 2
   × 6

52) 8
   × 2

53) 2
   × 3

54) 9
   × 2

55) 2
   × 8

56) 4
   × 2

57) 2
   × 4

58) 2
   × 2

59) 2
   × 7

60) 9
   × 2

Time
:

Score

/60

DAY 5
· Multiplying 2 ·

1)   2 × 4

2)   4 × 2

3)   2 × 7

4)   6 × 2

5)   2 × 9

6)   9 × 2

7)   2 × 9

8)   2 × 2

9)   2 × 6

10)   6 × 2

11)   2 × 7

12)   4 × 2

13)   2 × 7

14)   2 × 2

15)   2 × 4

16)   9 × 2

17)   2 × 2

18)   9 × 2

19)   2 × 6

20)   6 × 2

21)   2 × 6

22)   4 × 2

23)   2 × 9

24)   4 × 2

25)   2 × 8

26)   8 × 2

27)   2 × 6

28)   2 × 2

29)   2 × 5

30)   5 × 2

31)   2 × 9

32)   9 × 2

33)   2 × 2

34)   5 × 2

35)   2 × 4

36)   6 × 2

37)   2 × 2

38)   2 × 2

39)   2 × 4

40)   5 × 2

41)   2 × 9

42)   5 × 2

43)   2 × 6

44)   9 × 2

45)   2 × 9

46)   2 × 2

47)   2 × 6

48)   5 × 2

49)   2 × 5

50)   5 × 2

51)   2 × 2

52)   2 × 2

53)   2 × 3

54)   4 × 2

55)   2 × 7

56)   3 × 2

57)   2 × 8

58)   9 × 2

59)   2 × 4

60)   6 × 2

Time :

Score /60

DAY 6
· Multiplying 2 ·

1) 2 × 4
2) 5 × 2
3) 2 × 4
4) 2 × 2
5) 2 × 7
6) 9 × 2
7) 2 × 3

8) 8 × 2
9) 2 × 7
10) 1 × 2
11) 2 × 7
12) 5 × 2
13) 2 × 9
14) 7 × 2

15) 2 × 9
16) 6 × 2
17) 2 × 9
18) 5 × 2
19) 2 × 3
20) 5 × 2
21) 2 × 5

22) 8 × 2
23) 2 × 3
24) 5 × 2
25) 2 × 3
26) 5 × 2
27) 2 × 5
28) 4 × 2

29) 2 × 4
30) 2 × 2
31) 2 × 5
32) 4 × 2
33) 2 × 6
34) 7 × 2
35) 2 × 2

36) 0 × 2
37) 2 × 0
38) 6 × 2
39) 2 × 5
40) 8 × 2
41) 2 × 8
42) 2 × 2

43) 2 × 1
44) 2 × 2
45) 2 × 7
46) 6 × 2
47) 2 × 0
48) 9 × 2
49) 2 × 5

50) 4 × 2
51) 2 × 2
52) 9 × 2
53) 2 × 4
54) 9 × 2
55) 2 × 1
56) 4 × 2

57) 2 × 5
58) 3 × 2
59) 2 × 7
60) 3 × 2

Time :

Score /60

DAY 7
· Multiplying 2 ·

1)
$$\begin{array}{r} 2 \\ \times\ 5 \\ \hline \end{array}$$
2)
$$\begin{array}{r} 6 \\ \times\ 2 \\ \hline \end{array}$$
3)
$$\begin{array}{r} 2 \\ \times\ 2 \\ \hline \end{array}$$
4)
$$\begin{array}{r} 8 \\ \times\ 2 \\ \hline \end{array}$$
5)
$$\begin{array}{r} 2 \\ \times\ 2 \\ \hline \end{array}$$
6)
$$\begin{array}{r} 7 \\ \times\ 2 \\ \hline \end{array}$$
7)
$$\begin{array}{r} 2 \\ \times\ 5 \\ \hline \end{array}$$

8)
$$\begin{array}{r} 5 \\ \times\ 2 \\ \hline \end{array}$$
9)
$$\begin{array}{r} 2 \\ \times\ 7 \\ \hline \end{array}$$
10)
$$\begin{array}{r} 3 \\ \times\ 2 \\ \hline \end{array}$$
11)
$$\begin{array}{r} 2 \\ \times\ 5 \\ \hline \end{array}$$
12)
$$\begin{array}{r} 8 \\ \times\ 2 \\ \hline \end{array}$$
13)
$$\begin{array}{r} 2 \\ \times\ 9 \\ \hline \end{array}$$
14)
$$\begin{array}{r} 7 \\ \times\ 2 \\ \hline \end{array}$$

15)
$$\begin{array}{r} 2 \\ \times\ 5 \\ \hline \end{array}$$
16)
$$\begin{array}{r} 4 \\ \times\ 2 \\ \hline \end{array}$$
17)
$$\begin{array}{r} 2 \\ \times\ 3 \\ \hline \end{array}$$
18)
$$\begin{array}{r} 8 \\ \times\ 2 \\ \hline \end{array}$$
19)
$$\begin{array}{r} 2 \\ \times\ 4 \\ \hline \end{array}$$
20)
$$\begin{array}{r} 5 \\ \times\ 2 \\ \hline \end{array}$$
21)
$$\begin{array}{r} 2 \\ \times\ 3 \\ \hline \end{array}$$

22)
$$\begin{array}{r} 4 \\ \times\ 2 \\ \hline \end{array}$$
23)
$$\begin{array}{r} 2 \\ \times\ 9 \\ \hline \end{array}$$
24)
$$\begin{array}{r} 9 \\ \times\ 2 \\ \hline \end{array}$$
25)
$$\begin{array}{r} 2 \\ \times\ 5 \\ \hline \end{array}$$
26)
$$\begin{array}{r} 4 \\ \times\ 2 \\ \hline \end{array}$$
27)
$$\begin{array}{r} 2 \\ \times\ 3 \\ \hline \end{array}$$
28)
$$\begin{array}{r} 7 \\ \times\ 2 \\ \hline \end{array}$$

29)
$$\begin{array}{r} 2 \\ \times\ 8 \\ \hline \end{array}$$
30)
$$\begin{array}{r} 3 \\ \times\ 2 \\ \hline \end{array}$$
31)
$$\begin{array}{r} 2 \\ \times\ 2 \\ \hline \end{array}$$
32)
$$\begin{array}{r} 8 \\ \times\ 2 \\ \hline \end{array}$$
33)
$$\begin{array}{r} 2 \\ \times\ 2 \\ \hline \end{array}$$
34)
$$\begin{array}{r} 3 \\ \times\ 2 \\ \hline \end{array}$$
35)
$$\begin{array}{r} 2 \\ \times\ 3 \\ \hline \end{array}$$

36)
$$\begin{array}{r} 6 \\ \times\ 2 \\ \hline \end{array}$$
37)
$$\begin{array}{r} 2 \\ \times\ 7 \\ \hline \end{array}$$
38)
$$\begin{array}{r} 3 \\ \times\ 2 \\ \hline \end{array}$$
39)
$$\begin{array}{r} 2 \\ \times\ 9 \\ \hline \end{array}$$
40)
$$\begin{array}{r} 9 \\ \times\ 2 \\ \hline \end{array}$$
41)
$$\begin{array}{r} 2 \\ \times\ 8 \\ \hline \end{array}$$
42)
$$\begin{array}{r} 7 \\ \times\ 2 \\ \hline \end{array}$$

43)
$$\begin{array}{r} 2 \\ \times\ 2 \\ \hline \end{array}$$
44)
$$\begin{array}{r} 7 \\ \times\ 2 \\ \hline \end{array}$$
45)
$$\begin{array}{r} 2 \\ \times\ 7 \\ \hline \end{array}$$
46)
$$\begin{array}{r} 3 \\ \times\ 2 \\ \hline \end{array}$$
47)
$$\begin{array}{r} 2 \\ \times\ 9 \\ \hline \end{array}$$
48)
$$\begin{array}{r} 3 \\ \times\ 2 \\ \hline \end{array}$$
49)
$$\begin{array}{r} 2 \\ \times\ 9 \\ \hline \end{array}$$

50)
$$\begin{array}{r} 7 \\ \times\ 2 \\ \hline \end{array}$$
51)
$$\begin{array}{r} 2 \\ \times\ 5 \\ \hline \end{array}$$
52)
$$\begin{array}{r} 2 \\ \times\ 2 \\ \hline \end{array}$$
53)
$$\begin{array}{r} 2 \\ \times\ 9 \\ \hline \end{array}$$
54)
$$\begin{array}{r} 7 \\ \times\ 2 \\ \hline \end{array}$$
55)
$$\begin{array}{r} 2 \\ \times\ 4 \\ \hline \end{array}$$
56)
$$\begin{array}{r} 8 \\ \times\ 2 \\ \hline \end{array}$$

57)
$$\begin{array}{r} 2 \\ \times\ 4 \\ \hline \end{array}$$
58)
$$\begin{array}{r} 9 \\ \times\ 2 \\ \hline \end{array}$$
59)
$$\begin{array}{r} 2 \\ \times\ 6 \\ \hline \end{array}$$
60)
$$\begin{array}{r} 3 \\ \times\ 2 \\ \hline \end{array}$$

Time :

Score /60

DAY 8
· Multiplying 2 ·

1) 2 × 6

2) 10 × 2

3) 2 × 6

4) 3 × 2

5) 2 × 3

6) 2 × 2

7) 2 × 12

8) 12 × 2

9) 2 × 11

10) 3 × 2

11) 2 × 4

12) 7 × 2

13) 2 × 3

14) 8 × 2

15) 2 × 7

16) 7 × 2

17) 2 × 5

18) 10 × 2

19) 2 × 11

20) 10 × 2

21) 2 × 10

22) 10 × 2

23) 2 × 6

24) 4 × 2

25) 2 × 11

26) 9 × 2

27) 2 × 9

28) 3 × 2

29) 2 × 2

30) 6 × 2

31) 2 × 4

32) 5 × 2

33) 2 × 6

34) 2 × 2

35) 2 × 5

36) 8 × 2

37) 2 × 7

38) 8 × 2

39) 2 × 8

40) 5 × 2

41) 2 × 7

42) 2 × 2

43) 2 × 2

44) 5 × 2

45) 2 × 8

46) 5 × 2

47) 2 × 12

48) 11 × 2

49) 2 × 9

50) 4 × 2

51) 2 × 8

52) 6 × 2

53) 2 × 8

54) 7 × 2

55) 2 × 3

56) 3 × 2

57) 2 × 10

58) 9 × 2

59) 2 × 12

60) 6 × 2

Time :

Score /60

DAY 9
· Multiplying 2 ·

1)   2
  × 0

2)   11
  ×   2

3)   2
  × 6

4)   6
  × 2

5)   2
  × 7

6)   11
  ×   2

7)   2
  × 2

8)   9
  × 2

9)   2
  × 3

10)   12
  ×   2

11)   2
  × 6

12)   4
  × 2

13)   2
  × 2

14)   8
  × 2

15)   2
  × 2

16)   12
  ×   2

17)   2
  × 3

18)   11
  ×   2

19)   2
  × 3

20)   7
  × 2

21)   2
  × 5

22)   2
  × 2

23)   2
  × 7

24)   5
  × 2

25)   2
  × 8

26)   3
  × 2

27)   2
  × 2

28)   4
  × 2

29)   2
  × 11

30)   0
  × 2

31)   2
  × 9

32)   10
  ×   2

33)   2
  × 7

34)   2
  × 2

35)   2
  × 12

36)   1
  × 2

37)   2
  × 6

38)   4
  × 2

39)   2
  × 9

40)   1
  × 2

41)   2
  × 1

42)   7
  × 2

43)   2
  × 9

44)   5
  × 2

45)   2
  × 0

46)   5
  × 2

47)   2
  × 8

48)   8
  × 2

49)   2
  × 1

50)   7
  × 2

51)   2
  × 4

52)   4
  × 2

53)   2
  × 9

54)   9
  × 2

55)   2
  × 4

56)   4
  × 2

57)   2
  × 1

58)   7
  × 2

59)   2
  × 7

60)   12
  ×   2

Time
:

Score
/60

DAY 10

· Multiplying 2 ·

1) $\begin{array}{r} 2 \\ \times\ 11 \\ \hline \end{array}$ 2) $\begin{array}{r} 6 \\ \times\ 2 \\ \hline \end{array}$ 3) $\begin{array}{r} 2 \\ \times\ 4 \\ \hline \end{array}$ 4) $\begin{array}{r} 10 \\ \times\ 2 \\ \hline \end{array}$ 5) $\begin{array}{r} 2 \\ \times\ 10 \\ \hline \end{array}$ 6) $\begin{array}{r} 10 \\ \times\ 2 \\ \hline \end{array}$ 7) $\begin{array}{r} 2 \\ \times\ 7 \\ \hline \end{array}$

8) $\begin{array}{r} 4 \\ \times\ 2 \\ \hline \end{array}$ 9) $\begin{array}{r} 2 \\ \times\ 8 \\ \hline \end{array}$ 10) $\begin{array}{r} 11 \\ \times\ 2 \\ \hline \end{array}$ 11) $\begin{array}{r} 2 \\ \times\ 3 \\ \hline \end{array}$ 12) $\begin{array}{r} 4 \\ \times\ 2 \\ \hline \end{array}$ 13) $\begin{array}{r} 2 \\ \times\ 12 \\ \hline \end{array}$ 14) $\begin{array}{r} 12 \\ \times\ 2 \\ \hline \end{array}$

15) $\begin{array}{r} 2 \\ \times\ 6 \\ \hline \end{array}$ 16) $\begin{array}{r} 12 \\ \times\ 2 \\ \hline \end{array}$ 17) $\begin{array}{r} 2 \\ \times\ 3 \\ \hline \end{array}$ 18) $\begin{array}{r} 3 \\ \times\ 2 \\ \hline \end{array}$ 19) $\begin{array}{r} 2 \\ \times\ 6 \\ \hline \end{array}$ 20) $\begin{array}{r} 7 \\ \times\ 2 \\ \hline \end{array}$ 21) $\begin{array}{r} 2 \\ \times\ 11 \\ \hline \end{array}$

22) $\begin{array}{r} 11 \\ \times\ 2 \\ \hline \end{array}$ 23) $\begin{array}{r} 2 \\ \times\ 7 \\ \hline \end{array}$ 24) $\begin{array}{r} 7 \\ \times\ 2 \\ \hline \end{array}$ 25) $\begin{array}{r} 2 \\ \times\ 2 \\ \hline \end{array}$ 26) $\begin{array}{r} 12 \\ \times\ 2 \\ \hline \end{array}$ 27) $\begin{array}{r} 2 \\ \times\ 12 \\ \hline \end{array}$ 28) $\begin{array}{r} 2 \\ \times\ 2 \\ \hline \end{array}$

29) $\begin{array}{r} 2 \\ \times\ 10 \\ \hline \end{array}$ 30) $\begin{array}{r} 12 \\ \times\ 2 \\ \hline \end{array}$ 31) $\begin{array}{r} 2 \\ \times\ 2 \\ \hline \end{array}$ 32) $\begin{array}{r} 11 \\ \times\ 2 \\ \hline \end{array}$ 33) $\begin{array}{r} 2 \\ \times\ 5 \\ \hline \end{array}$ 34) $\begin{array}{r} 4 \\ \times\ 2 \\ \hline \end{array}$ 35) $\begin{array}{r} 2 \\ \times\ 9 \\ \hline \end{array}$

36) $\begin{array}{r} 12 \\ \times\ 2 \\ \hline \end{array}$ 37) $\begin{array}{r} 2 \\ \times\ 7 \\ \hline \end{array}$ 38) $\begin{array}{r} 10 \\ \times\ 2 \\ \hline \end{array}$ 39) $\begin{array}{r} 2 \\ \times\ 12 \\ \hline \end{array}$ 40) $\begin{array}{r} 7 \\ \times\ 2 \\ \hline \end{array}$ 41) $\begin{array}{r} 2 \\ \times\ 10 \\ \hline \end{array}$ 42) $\begin{array}{r} 6 \\ \times\ 2 \\ \hline \end{array}$

43) $\begin{array}{r} 2 \\ \times\ 9 \\ \hline \end{array}$ 44) $\begin{array}{r} 6 \\ \times\ 2 \\ \hline \end{array}$ 45) $\begin{array}{r} 2 \\ \times\ 11 \\ \hline \end{array}$ 46) $\begin{array}{r} 3 \\ \times\ 2 \\ \hline \end{array}$ 47) $\begin{array}{r} 2 \\ \times\ 8 \\ \hline \end{array}$ 48) $\begin{array}{r} 6 \\ \times\ 2 \\ \hline \end{array}$ 49) $\begin{array}{r} 2 \\ \times\ 9 \\ \hline \end{array}$

50) $\begin{array}{r} 11 \\ \times\ 2 \\ \hline \end{array}$ 51) $\begin{array}{r} 2 \\ \times\ 10 \\ \hline \end{array}$ 52) $\begin{array}{r} 12 \\ \times\ 2 \\ \hline \end{array}$ 53) $\begin{array}{r} 2 \\ \times\ 4 \\ \hline \end{array}$ 54) $\begin{array}{r} 7 \\ \times\ 2 \\ \hline \end{array}$ 55) $\begin{array}{r} 2 \\ \times\ 8 \\ \hline \end{array}$ 56) $\begin{array}{r} 6 \\ \times\ 2 \\ \hline \end{array}$

57) $\begin{array}{r} 2 \\ \times\ 10 \\ \hline \end{array}$ 58) $\begin{array}{r} 9 \\ \times\ 2 \\ \hline \end{array}$ 59) $\begin{array}{r} 2 \\ \times\ 12 \\ \hline \end{array}$ 60) $\begin{array}{r} 10 \\ \times\ 2 \\ \hline \end{array}$

Time
:

Score

/60

DAY 11
· Multiplying 2 ·

1) $\begin{array}{r} 2 \\ \times\ 7 \\ \hline \end{array}$ 2) $\begin{array}{r} 12 \\ \times\ 2 \\ \hline \end{array}$ 3) $\begin{array}{r} 2 \\ \times\ 6 \\ \hline \end{array}$ 4) $\begin{array}{r} 2 \\ \times\ 2 \\ \hline \end{array}$ 5) $\begin{array}{r} 2 \\ \times\ 10 \\ \hline \end{array}$ 6) $\begin{array}{r} 8 \\ \times\ 2 \\ \hline \end{array}$ 7) $\begin{array}{r} 2 \\ \times\ 7 \\ \hline \end{array}$

8) $\begin{array}{r} 7 \\ \times\ 2 \\ \hline \end{array}$ 9) $\begin{array}{r} 2 \\ \times\ 6 \\ \hline \end{array}$ 10) $\begin{array}{r} 5 \\ \times\ 2 \\ \hline \end{array}$ 11) $\begin{array}{r} 2 \\ \times\ 10 \\ \hline \end{array}$ 12) $\begin{array}{r} 5 \\ \times\ 2 \\ \hline \end{array}$ 13) $\begin{array}{r} 2 \\ \times\ 5 \\ \hline \end{array}$ 14) $\begin{array}{r} 2 \\ \times\ 2 \\ \hline \end{array}$

15) $\begin{array}{r} 2 \\ \times\ 2 \\ \hline \end{array}$ 16) $\begin{array}{r} 3 \\ \times\ 2 \\ \hline \end{array}$ 17) $\begin{array}{r} 2 \\ \times\ 3 \\ \hline \end{array}$ 18) $\begin{array}{r} 10 \\ \times\ 2 \\ \hline \end{array}$ 19) $\begin{array}{r} 2 \\ \times\ 9 \\ \hline \end{array}$ 20) $\begin{array}{r} 8 \\ \times\ 2 \\ \hline \end{array}$ 21) $\begin{array}{r} 2 \\ \times\ 4 \\ \hline \end{array}$

22) $\begin{array}{r} 10 \\ \times\ 2 \\ \hline \end{array}$ 23) $\begin{array}{r} 2 \\ \times\ 6 \\ \hline \end{array}$ 24) $\begin{array}{r} 7 \\ \times\ 2 \\ \hline \end{array}$ 25) $\begin{array}{r} 2 \\ \times\ 2 \\ \hline \end{array}$ 26) $\begin{array}{r} 11 \\ \times\ 2 \\ \hline \end{array}$ 27) $\begin{array}{r} 2 \\ \times\ 12 \\ \hline \end{array}$ 28) $\begin{array}{r} 8 \\ \times\ 2 \\ \hline \end{array}$

29) $\begin{array}{r} 2 \\ \times\ 4 \\ \hline \end{array}$ 30) $\begin{array}{r} 12 \\ \times\ 2 \\ \hline \end{array}$ 31) $\begin{array}{r} 2 \\ \times\ 5 \\ \hline \end{array}$ 32) $\begin{array}{r} 2 \\ \times\ 2 \\ \hline \end{array}$ 33) $\begin{array}{r} 2 \\ \times\ 7 \\ \hline \end{array}$ 34) $\begin{array}{r} 9 \\ \times\ 2 \\ \hline \end{array}$ 35) $\begin{array}{r} 2 \\ \times\ 9 \\ \hline \end{array}$

36) $\begin{array}{r} 11 \\ \times\ 2 \\ \hline \end{array}$ 37) $\begin{array}{r} 2 \\ \times\ 5 \\ \hline \end{array}$ 38) $\begin{array}{r} 7 \\ \times\ 2 \\ \hline \end{array}$ 39) $\begin{array}{r} 2 \\ \times\ 2 \\ \hline \end{array}$ 40) $\begin{array}{r} 2 \\ \times\ 2 \\ \hline \end{array}$ 41) $\begin{array}{r} 2 \\ \times\ 3 \\ \hline \end{array}$ 42) $\begin{array}{r} 7 \\ \times\ 2 \\ \hline \end{array}$

43) $\begin{array}{r} 2 \\ \times\ 2 \\ \hline \end{array}$ 44) $\begin{array}{r} 8 \\ \times\ 2 \\ \hline \end{array}$ 45) $\begin{array}{r} 2 \\ \times\ 5 \\ \hline \end{array}$ 46) $\begin{array}{r} 4 \\ \times\ 2 \\ \hline \end{array}$ 47) $\begin{array}{r} 2 \\ \times\ 7 \\ \hline \end{array}$ 48) $\begin{array}{r} 9 \\ \times\ 2 \\ \hline \end{array}$ 49) $\begin{array}{r} 2 \\ \times\ 5 \\ \hline \end{array}$

50) $\begin{array}{r} 8 \\ \times\ 2 \\ \hline \end{array}$ 51) $\begin{array}{r} 2 \\ \times\ 4 \\ \hline \end{array}$ 52) $\begin{array}{r} 6 \\ \times\ 2 \\ \hline \end{array}$ 53) $\begin{array}{r} 2 \\ \times\ 8 \\ \hline \end{array}$ 54) $\begin{array}{r} 2 \\ \times\ 2 \\ \hline \end{array}$ 55) $\begin{array}{r} 2 \\ \times\ 5 \\ \hline \end{array}$ 56) $\begin{array}{r} 9 \\ \times\ 2 \\ \hline \end{array}$

57) $\begin{array}{r} 2 \\ \times\ 7 \\ \hline \end{array}$ 58) $\begin{array}{r} 4 \\ \times\ 2 \\ \hline \end{array}$ 59) $\begin{array}{r} 2 \\ \times\ 6 \\ \hline \end{array}$ 60) $\begin{array}{r} 10 \\ \times\ 2 \\ \hline \end{array}$

Time :

Score /60

111111111 x 111111111 = 123456789987654321

This is one that's sure to impress your friends, math teachers, or both! There are some seriously big numbers here, and a lot of ones.

This cool trick actually works with any amount of 1s up to 9, so you can also use 11 x 11, or 111 x 111, or 1111 x 1111, and so on. You'll always get an answer that has numbers ascending at the start and descending at the end, like 12321.

Once you get to 10 1s (1111111111 x 1111111111) you end up with some zeroes in the middle and it starts to get a bit messy, like the ground when I start digging up another fact!

DAY 12

· Multiplying 3 ·

1)   3
× 8

2)   7
× 3

3)   3
× 6

4)   5
× 3

5)   3
× 5

6)   9
× 3

7)   3
× 7

8)   5
× 3

9)   3
× 6

10)   6
× 3

11)   3
× 9

12)   8
× 3

13)   3
× 4

14)   5
× 3

15)   3
× 2

16)   5
× 3

17)   3
× 2

18)   6
× 3

19)   3
× 8

20)   8
× 3

21)   3
× 4

22)   7
× 3

23)   3
× 4

24)   9
× 3

25)   3
× 7

26)   5
× 3

27)   3
× 8

28)   4
× 3

29)   3
× 7

30)   3
× 3

31)   3
× 9

32)   5
× 3

33)   3
× 4

34)   4
× 3

35)   3
× 3

36)   9
× 3

37)   3
× 7

38)   6
× 3

39)   3
× 5

40)   7
× 3

41)   3
× 9

42)   7
× 3

43)   3
× 2

44)   8
× 3

45)   3
× 9

46)   7
× 3

47)   3
× 5

48)   4
× 3

49)   3
× 4

50)   7
× 3

51)   3
× 4

52)   2
× 3

53)   3
× 2

54)   8
× 3

55)   3
× 4

56)   9
× 3

57)   3
× 9

58)   9
× 3

59)   3
× 3

60)   9
× 3

Time
:

Score
/60

DAY 13

· Multiplying 3 ·

1) 3 × 8

2) 5 × 3

3) 3 × 7

4) 5 × 3

5) 3 × 3

6) 8 × 3

7) 3 × 4

8) 4 × 3

9) 3 × 8

10) 5 × 3

11) 3 × 7

12) 2 × 3

13) 3 × 9

14) 7 × 3

15) 3 × 7

16) 8 × 3

17) 3 × 6

18) 6 × 3

19) 3 × 4

20) 5 × 3

21) 3 × 2

22) 9 × 3

23) 3 × 6

24) 9 × 3

25) 3 × 2

26) 4 × 3

27) 3 × 7

28) 6 × 3

29) 3 × 7

30) 6 × 3

31) 3 × 5

32) 3 × 3

33) 3 × 4

34) 4 × 3

35) 3 × 3

36) 9 × 3

37) 3 × 5

38) 2 × 3

39) 3 × 8

40) 9 × 3

41) 3 × 6

42) 8 × 3

43) 3 × 5

44) 6 × 3

45) 3 × 9

46) 6 × 3

47) 3 × 6

48) 2 × 3

49) 3 × 4

50) 5 × 3

51) 3 × 4

52) 5 × 3

53) 3 × 6

54) 4 × 3

55) 3 × 5

56) 6 × 3

57) 3 × 2

58) 2 × 3

59) 3 × 8

60) 4 × 3

Time :

Score /60

DAY 14
· Multiplying 3 ·

1) 3 × 9
2) 7 × 3
3) 3 × 8
4) 1 × 3
5) 3 × 2
6) 4 × 3
7) 3 × 2

8) 0 × 3
9) 3 × 5
10) 4 × 3
11) 3 × 6
12) 0 × 3
13) 3 × 3
14) 8 × 3

15) 3 × 6
16) 4 × 3
17) 3 × 9
18) 8 × 3
19) 3 × 6
20) 2 × 3
21) 3 × 6

22) 4 × 3
23) 3 × 8
24) 0 × 3
25) 3 × 4
26) 7 × 3
27) 3 × 2
28) 2 × 3

29) 3 × 8
30) 7 × 3
31) 3 × 7
32) 4 × 3
33) 3 × 1
34) 6 × 3
35) 3 × 7

36) 1 × 3
37) 3 × 2
38) 3 × 3
39) 3 × 5
40) 6 × 3
41) 3 × 6
42) 8 × 3

43) 3 × 9
44) 6 × 3
45) 3 × 8
46) 6 × 3
47) 3 × 3
48) 0 × 3
49) 3 × 1

50) 1 × 3
51) 3 × 2
52) 1 × 3
53) 3 × 8
54) 2 × 3
55) 3 × 9
56) 8 × 3

57) 3 × 7
58) 1 × 3
59) 3 × 8
60) 4 × 3

Time :

Score /60

DAY 15
· Multiplying 3 ·

1) 3 × 7

2) 9 × 3

3) 3 × 7

4) 9 × 3

5) 3 × 5

6) 4 × 3

7) 3 × 3

8) 2 × 3

9) 3 × 7

10) 7 × 3

11) 3 × 7

12) 6 × 3

13) 3 × 7

14) 4 × 3

15) 3 × 4

16) 7 × 3

17) 3 × 5

18) 7 × 3

19) 3 × 2

20) 4 × 3

21) 3 × 3

22) 8 × 3

23) 3 × 6

24) 2 × 3

25) 3 × 8

26) 9 × 3

27) 3 × 6

28) 9 × 3

29) 3 × 9

30) 2 × 3

31) 3 × 8

32) 2 × 3

33) 3 × 9

34) 2 × 3

35) 3 × 5

36) 6 × 3

37) 3 × 6

38) 6 × 3

39) 3 × 9

40) 6 × 3

41) 3 × 2

42) 7 × 3

43) 3 × 7

44) 3 × 3

45) 3 × 3

46) 8 × 3

47) 3 × 4

48) 7 × 3

49) 3 × 3

50) 8 × 3

51) 3 × 8

52) 8 × 3

53) 3 × 8

54) 9 × 3

55) 3 × 9

56) 2 × 3

57) 3 × 6

58) 9 × 3

59) 3 × 5

60) 4 × 3

Time :

Score /60

DAY 16
· Multiplying 3 ·

1)
```
    3
×  12
```
2)
```
    5
×   3
```
3)
```
    3
×   1
```
4)
```
    2
×   3
```
5)
```
    3
×   7
```
6)
```
    4
×   3
```
7)
```
    3
×   3
```

8)
```
    6
×   3
```
9)
```
    3
×   4
```
10)
```
   12
×   3
```
11)
```
    3
×  11
```
12)
```
    4
×   3
```
13)
```
    3
×  10
```
14)
```
    6
×   3
```

15)
```
    3
×   0
```
16)
```
    3
×   3
```
17)
```
    3
×   6
```
18)
```
    9
×   3
```
19)
```
    3
×   9
```
20)
```
    6
×   3
```
21)
```
    3
×   8
```

22)
```
   12
×   3
```
23)
```
    3
×   6
```
24)
```
    7
×   3
```
25)
```
    3
×   6
```
26)
```
    4
×   3
```
27)
```
    3
×   8
```
28)
```
    8
×   3
```

29)
```
    3
×   7
```
30)
```
    5
×   3
```
31)
```
    3
×   5
```
32)
```
    4
×   3
```
33)
```
    3
×   6
```
34)
```
   11
×   3
```
35)
```
    3
×  12
```

36)
```
    9
×   3
```
37)
```
    3
×  12
```
38)
```
    6
×   3
```
39)
```
    3
×   3
```
40)
```
    2
×   3
```
41)
```
    3
×   7
```
42)
```
    1
×   3
```

43)
```
    3
×   0
```
44)
```
    1
×   3
```
45)
```
    3
×   6
```
46)
```
    9
×   3
```
47)
```
    3
×   6
```
48)
```
   10
×   3
```
49)
```
    3
×   5
```

50)
```
   10
×   3
```
51)
```
    3
×   6
```
52)
```
    3
×   3
```
53)
```
    3
×   3
```
54)
```
    3
×   3
```
55)
```
    3
×   1
```
56)
```
    4
×   3
```

57)
```
    3
×   1
```
58)
```
    2
×   3
```
59)
```
    3
×   9
```
60)
```
    2
×   3
```

Time
:

Score
/60

DAY 17

· Multiplying 3 ·

1) 3 × 9

2) 3 × 3

3) 3 × 12

4) 11 × 3

5) 3 × 10

6) 10 × 3

7) 3 × 3

8) 10 × 3

9) 3 × 11

10) 7 × 3

11) 3 × 8

12) 10 × 3

13) 3 × 5

14) 7 × 3

15) 3 × 5

16) 11 × 3

17) 3 × 7

18) 3 × 3

19) 3 × 9

20) 2 × 3

21) 3 × 10

22) 9 × 3

23) 3 × 6

24) 11 × 3

25) 3 × 4

26) 6 × 3

27) 3 × 10

28) 8 × 3

29) 3 × 2

30) 10 × 3

31) 3 × 6

32) 12 × 3

33) 3 × 10

34) 9 × 3

35) 3 × 7

36) 11 × 3

37) 3 × 8

38) 5 × 3

39) 3 × 7

40) 10 × 3

41) 3 × 4

42) 8 × 3

43) 3 × 5

44) 6 × 3

45) 3 × 9

46) 2 × 3

47) 3 × 10

48) 9 × 3

49) 3 × 7

50) 8 × 3

51) 3 × 10

52) 8 × 3

53) 3 × 8

54) 9 × 3

55) 3 × 3

56) 8 × 3

57) 3 × 8

58) 3 × 3

59) 3 × 4

60) 5 × 3

Time :

Score /60

DAY 18

· Multiplying 3 ·

1)
```
    3
×   2
```

2)
```
   12
×   3
```

3)
```
    3
×  11
```

4)
```
    5
×   3
```

5)
```
    3
×  12
```

6)
```
   11
×   3
```

7)
```
    3
×  11
```

8)
```
    4
×   3
```

9)
```
    3
×   6
```

10)
```
    2
×   3
```

11)
```
    3
×  12
```

12)
```
    9
×   3
```

13)
```
    3
×   5
```

14)
```
    7
×   3
```

15)
```
    3
×   7
```

16)
```
    7
×   3
```

17)
```
    3
×  11
```

18)
```
    4
×   3
```

19)
```
    3
×   6
```

20)
```
    4
×   3
```

21)
```
    3
×   4
```

22)
```
    4
×   3
```

23)
```
    3
×   4
```

24)
```
   10
×   3
```

25)
```
    3
×   8
```

26)
```
    2
×   3
```

27)
```
    3
×  10
```

28)
```
    3
×   3
```

29)
```
    3
×   8
```

30)
```
   10
×   3
```

31)
```
    3
×   3
```

32)
```
    6
×   3
```

33)
```
    3
×   7
```

34)
```
    5
×   3
```

35)
```
    3
×   6
```

36)
```
    9
×   3
```

37)
```
    3
×   4
```

38)
```
    8
×   3
```

39)
```
    3
×  10
```

40)
```
    5
×   3
```

41)
```
    3
×   9
```

42)
```
    8
×   3
```

43)
```
    3
×   5
```

44)
```
   10
×   3
```

45)
```
    3
×   5
```

46)
```
    9
×   3
```

47)
```
    3
×  12
```

48)
```
    5
×   3
```

49)
```
    3
×   2
```

50)
```
    7
×   3
```

51)
```
    3
×   6
```

52)
```
    6
×   3
```

53)
```
    3
×   9
```

54)
```
    7
×   3
```

55)
```
    3
×  11
```

56)
```
    6
×   3
```

57)
```
    3
×   2
```

58)
```
    8
×   3
```

59)
```
    3
×   4
```

60)
```
    7
×   3
```

Time

:

Score

/60

DAY 19
· Multiplying 3 ·

1)   3
   × 6

2)   8
   × 3

3)   3
   × 2

4)   8
   × 3

5)   3
   × 3

6)   2
   × 3

7)   3
   × 4

8)   10
   × 3

9)   3
   × 2

10)   4
   × 3

11)   3
   × 10

12)   5
   × 3

13)   3
   × 3

14)   9
   × 3

15)   3
   × 5

16)   10
   × 3

17)   3
   × 8

18)   5
   × 3

19)   3
   × 5

20)   10
   × 3

21)   3
   × 5

22)   4
   × 3

23)   3
   × 10

24)   10
   × 3

25)   3
   × 11

26)   12
   × 3

27)   3
   × 11

28)   9
   × 3

29)   3
   × 11

30)   9
   × 3

31)   3
   × 10

32)   3
   × 3

33)   3
   × 3

34)   12
   × 3

35)   3
   × 6

36)   6
   × 3

37)   3
   × 2

38)   3
   × 3

39)   3
   × 10

40)   9
   × 3

41)   3
   × 8

42)   10
   × 3

43)   3
   × 4

44)   7
   × 3

45)   3
   × 2

46)   4
   × 3

47)   3
   × 7

48)   7
   × 3

49)   3
   × 2

50)   6
   × 3

51)   3
   × 6

52)   6
   × 3

53)   3
   × 8

54)   12
   × 3

55)   3
   × 11

56)   5
   × 3

57)   3
   × 9

58)   5
   × 3

59)   3
   × 12

60)   12
   × 3

Time
:

Score

/60

HERE'S A FUN MULTIPLICATION FACT USING THE NUMBER 3!

Take any number and multiply it by 3, then add together the digits in that number. You will always end up with a number divisible by three. Isn't that awesome!

For example:

8 x 3 = 24

2 + 4 = 6

6 / 3 = 2

DAY 20

· Multiplying 4 ·

1)   4
   × 3

2)   0
   × 4

3)   4
   × 5

4)   5
   × 4

5)   4
   × 6

6)   8
   × 4

7)   4
   × 4

8)   9
   × 4

9)   4
   × 1

10)   5
   × 4

11)   4
   × 4

12)   0
   × 4

13)   4
   × 2

14)   3
   × 4

15)   4
   × 8

16)   8
   × 4

17)   4
   × 2

18)   5
   × 4

19)   4
   × 8

20)   3
   × 4

21)   4
   × 7

22)   9
   × 4

23)   4
   × 0

24)   3
   × 4

25)   4
   × 2

26)   5
   × 4

27)   4
   × 2

28)   5
   × 4

29)   4
   × 0

30)   7
   × 4

31)   4
   × 3

32)   0
   × 4

33)   4
   × 2

34)   7
   × 4

35)   4
   × 8

36)   6
   × 4

37)   4
   × 7

38)   3
   × 4

39)   4
   × 1

40)   6
   × 4

41)   4
   × 4

42)   2
   × 4

43)   4
   × 6

44)   7
   × 4

45)   4
   × 5

46)   5
   × 4

47)   4
   × 8

48)   2
   × 4

49)   4
   × 7

50)   4
   × 4

51)   4
   × 9

52)   1
   × 4

53)   4
   × 6

54)   9
   × 4

55)   4
   × 0

56)   7
   × 4

57)   4
   × 3

58)   9
   × 4

59)   4
   × 6

60)   5
   × 4

Time :

Score

/60

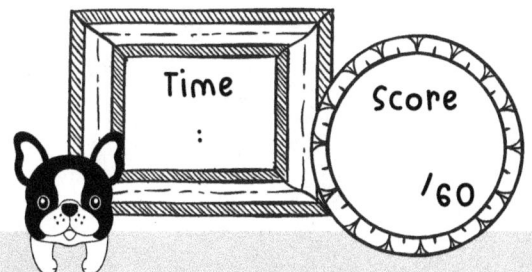

DAY 21
· Multiplying 4 ·

1) 4 × 8

2) 9 × 4

3) 4 × 3

4) 6 × 4

5) 4 × 5

6) 4 × 4

7) 4 × 3

8) 3 × 4

9) 4 × 5

10) 9 × 4

11) 4 × 7

12) 7 × 4

13) 4 × 2

14) 7 × 4

15) 4 × 9

16) 4 × 4

17) 4 × 9

18) 3 × 4

19) 4 × 6

20) 4 × 4

21) 4 × 5

22) 8 × 4

23) 4 × 8

24) 2 × 4

25) 4 × 6

26) 2 × 4

27) 4 × 3

28) 6 × 4

29) 4 × 2

30) 8 × 4

31) 4 × 9

32) 6 × 4

33) 4 × 4

34) 3 × 4

35) 4 × 8

36) 2 × 4

37) 4 × 9

38) 8 × 4

39) 4 × 8

40) 7 × 4

41) 4 × 8

42) 5 × 4

43) 4 × 9

44) 4 × 4

45) 4 × 7

46) 8 × 4

47) 4 × 7

48) 2 × 4

49) 4 × 6

50) 4 × 4

51) 4 × 9

52) 5 × 4

53) 4 × 5

54) 7 × 4

55) 4 × 3

56) 9 × 4

57) 4 × 3

58) 8 × 4

59) 4 × 7

60) 3 × 4

Time :

Score /60

DAY 22

· Multiplying 4 ·

1) 4
 × 7

2) 6
 × 4

3) 4
 × 2

4) 6
 × 4

5) 4
 × 7

6) 7
 × 4

7) 4
 × 9

8) 4
 × 4

9) 4
 × 7

10) 4
 × 4

11) 4
 × 9

12) 2
 × 4

13) 4
 × 3

14) 5
 × 4

15) 4
 × 2

16) 9
 × 4

17) 4
 × 7

18) 5
 × 4

19) 4
 × 7

20) 3
 × 4

21) 4
 × 6

22) 5
 × 4

23) 4
 × 8

24) 2
 × 4

25) 4
 × 6

26) 2
 × 4

27) 4
 × 9

28) 6
 × 4

29) 4
 × 8

30) 8
 × 4

31) 4
 × 5

32) 5
 × 4

33) 4
 × 9

34) 4
 × 4

35) 4
 × 3

36) 9
 × 4

37) 4
 × 8

38) 3
 × 4

39) 4
 × 7

40) 9
 × 4

41) 4
 × 6

42) 5
 × 4

43) 4
 × 2

44) 6
 × 4

45) 4
 × 3

46) 6
 × 4

47) 4
 × 8

48) 8
 × 4

49) 4
 × 9

50) 6
 × 4

51) 4
 × 8

52) 2
 × 4

53) 4
 × 8

54) 5
 × 4

55) 4
 × 6

56) 3
 × 4

57) 4
 × 7

58) 3
 × 4

59) 4
 × 2

60) 7
 × 4

Time
:

Score

/60

DAY 23
· Multiplying 4 ·

1) $\begin{array}{r} 4 \\ \times\ 9 \\ \hline \end{array}$
2) $\begin{array}{r} 4 \\ \times\ 4 \\ \hline \end{array}$
3) $\begin{array}{r} 4 \\ \times\ 9 \\ \hline \end{array}$
4) $\begin{array}{r} 5 \\ \times\ 4 \\ \hline \end{array}$
5) $\begin{array}{r} 4 \\ \times\ 9 \\ \hline \end{array}$
6) $\begin{array}{r} 9 \\ \times\ 4 \\ \hline \end{array}$
7) $\begin{array}{r} 4 \\ \times\ 9 \\ \hline \end{array}$

8) $\begin{array}{r} 2 \\ \times\ 4 \\ \hline \end{array}$
9) $\begin{array}{r} 4 \\ \times\ 9 \\ \hline \end{array}$
10) $\begin{array}{r} 8 \\ \times\ 4 \\ \hline \end{array}$
11) $\begin{array}{r} 4 \\ \times\ 5 \\ \hline \end{array}$
12) $\begin{array}{r} 8 \\ \times\ 4 \\ \hline \end{array}$
13) $\begin{array}{r} 4 \\ \times\ 9 \\ \hline \end{array}$
14) $\begin{array}{r} 4 \\ \times\ 4 \\ \hline \end{array}$

15) $\begin{array}{r} 4 \\ \times\ 2 \\ \hline \end{array}$
16) $\begin{array}{r} 6 \\ \times\ 4 \\ \hline \end{array}$
17) $\begin{array}{r} 4 \\ \times\ 7 \\ \hline \end{array}$
18) $\begin{array}{r} 4 \\ \times\ 4 \\ \hline \end{array}$
19) $\begin{array}{r} 4 \\ \times\ 7 \\ \hline \end{array}$
20) $\begin{array}{r} 7 \\ \times\ 4 \\ \hline \end{array}$
21) $\begin{array}{r} 4 \\ \times\ 4 \\ \hline \end{array}$

22) $\begin{array}{r} 9 \\ \times\ 4 \\ \hline \end{array}$
23) $\begin{array}{r} 4 \\ \times\ 5 \\ \hline \end{array}$
24) $\begin{array}{r} 9 \\ \times\ 4 \\ \hline \end{array}$
25) $\begin{array}{r} 4 \\ \times\ 2 \\ \hline \end{array}$
26) $\begin{array}{r} 7 \\ \times\ 4 \\ \hline \end{array}$
27) $\begin{array}{r} 4 \\ \times\ 6 \\ \hline \end{array}$
28) $\begin{array}{r} 2 \\ \times\ 4 \\ \hline \end{array}$

29) $\begin{array}{r} 4 \\ \times\ 7 \\ \hline \end{array}$
30) $\begin{array}{r} 2 \\ \times\ 4 \\ \hline \end{array}$
31) $\begin{array}{r} 4 \\ \times\ 5 \\ \hline \end{array}$
32) $\begin{array}{r} 9 \\ \times\ 4 \\ \hline \end{array}$
33) $\begin{array}{r} 4 \\ \times\ 9 \\ \hline \end{array}$
34) $\begin{array}{r} 9 \\ \times\ 4 \\ \hline \end{array}$
35) $\begin{array}{r} 4 \\ \times\ 9 \\ \hline \end{array}$

36) $\begin{array}{r} 6 \\ \times\ 4 \\ \hline \end{array}$
37) $\begin{array}{r} 4 \\ \times\ 4 \\ \hline \end{array}$
38) $\begin{array}{r} 8 \\ \times\ 4 \\ \hline \end{array}$
39) $\begin{array}{r} 4 \\ \times\ 5 \\ \hline \end{array}$
40) $\begin{array}{r} 5 \\ \times\ 4 \\ \hline \end{array}$
41) $\begin{array}{r} 4 \\ \times\ 6 \\ \hline \end{array}$
42) $\begin{array}{r} 8 \\ \times\ 4 \\ \hline \end{array}$

43) $\begin{array}{r} 4 \\ \times\ 6 \\ \hline \end{array}$
44) $\begin{array}{r} 9 \\ \times\ 4 \\ \hline \end{array}$
45) $\begin{array}{r} 4 \\ \times\ 9 \\ \hline \end{array}$
46) $\begin{array}{r} 5 \\ \times\ 4 \\ \hline \end{array}$
47) $\begin{array}{r} 4 \\ \times\ 2 \\ \hline \end{array}$
48) $\begin{array}{r} 2 \\ \times\ 4 \\ \hline \end{array}$
49) $\begin{array}{r} 4 \\ \times\ 6 \\ \hline \end{array}$

50) $\begin{array}{r} 6 \\ \times\ 4 \\ \hline \end{array}$
51) $\begin{array}{r} 4 \\ \times\ 5 \\ \hline \end{array}$
52) $\begin{array}{r} 9 \\ \times\ 4 \\ \hline \end{array}$
53) $\begin{array}{r} 4 \\ \times\ 4 \\ \hline \end{array}$
54) $\begin{array}{r} 7 \\ \times\ 4 \\ \hline \end{array}$
55) $\begin{array}{r} 4 \\ \times\ 2 \\ \hline \end{array}$
56) $\begin{array}{r} 8 \\ \times\ 4 \\ \hline \end{array}$

57) $\begin{array}{r} 4 \\ \times\ 8 \\ \hline \end{array}$
58) $\begin{array}{r} 2 \\ \times\ 4 \\ \hline \end{array}$
59) $\begin{array}{r} 4 \\ \times\ 2 \\ \hline \end{array}$
60) $\begin{array}{r} 8 \\ \times\ 4 \\ \hline \end{array}$

Time

:

Score

/60

DAY 24
· Multiplying 4 ·

1) 4 × 3

2) 9 × 4

3) 4 × 11

4) 11 × 4

5) 4 × 10

6) 6 × 4

7) 4 × 5

8) 3 × 4

9) 4 × 9

10) 8 × 4

11) 4 × 6

12) 11 × 4

13) 4 × 3

14) 12 × 4

15) 4 × 3

16) 12 × 4

17) 4 × 4

18) 6 × 4

19) 4 × 11

20) 7 × 4

21) 4 × 3

22) 6 × 4

23) 4 × 5

24) 8 × 4

25) 4 × 11

26) 7 × 4

27) 4 × 8

28) 4 × 4

29) 4 × 12

30) 5 × 4

31) 4 × 7

32) 9 × 4

33) 4 × 5

34) 3 × 4

35) 4 × 9

36) 7 × 4

37) 4 × 3

38) 7 × 4

39) 4 × 5

40) 6 × 4

41) 4 × 8

42) 5 × 4

43) 4 × 8

44) 7 × 4

45) 4 × 2

46) 2 × 4

47) 4 × 4

48) 10 × 4

49) 4 × 11

50) 4 × 4

51) 4 × 12

52) 8 × 4

53) 4 × 9

54) 8 × 4

55) 4 × 11

56) 7 × 4

57) 4 × 10

58) 3 × 4

59) 4 × 12

60) 4 × 4

Time :

Score /60

DAY 25
· Multiplying 4 ·

1) 4 × 11

2) 8 × 4

3) 4 × 4

4) 12 × 4

5) 4 × 4

6) 12 × 4

7) 4 × 5

8) 1 × 4

9) 4 × 1

10) 0 × 4

11) 4 × 3

12) 6 × 4

13) 4 × 7

14) 12 × 4

15) 4 × 9

16) 2 × 4

17) 4 × 7

18) 12 × 4

19) 4 × 9

20) 5 × 4

21) 4 × 2

22) 1 × 4

23) 4 × 8

24) 8 × 4

25) 4 × 1

26) 6 × 4

27) 4 × 0

28) 9 × 4

29) 4 × 12

30) 5 × 4

31) 4 × 6

32) 9 × 4

33) 4 × 7

34) 6 × 4

35) 4 × 2

36) 1 × 4

37) 4 × 5

38) 11 × 4

39) 4 × 6

40) 7 × 4

41) 4 × 11

42) 10 × 4

43) 4 × 8

44) 4 × 4

45) 4 × 9

46) 6 × 4

47) 4 × 11

48) 12 × 4

49) 4 × 9

50) 9 × 4

51) 4 × 8

52) 7 × 4

53) 4 × 3

54) 4 × 4

55) 4 × 4

56) 11 × 4

57) 4 × 2

58) 3 × 4

59) 4 × 4

60) 3 × 4

Time :

Score /60

DAY 26

· Multiplying 4 ·

1)
```
    4
×   5
```
2)
```
   11
×   4
```
3)
```
    4
×  11
```
4)
```
    6
×   4
```
5)
```
    4
×   5
```
6)
```
    6
×   4
```
7)
```
    4
×  10
```

8)
```
   11
×   4
```
9)
```
    4
×  10
```
10)
```
    4
×   4
```
11)
```
    4
×   3
```
12)
```
    9
×   4
```
13)
```
    4
×  10
```
14)
```
    8
×   4
```

15)
```
    4
×   5
```
16)
```
    4
×   4
```
17)
```
    4
×   2
```
18)
```
    6
×   4
```
19)
```
    4
×   5
```
20)
```
    6
×   4
```
21)
```
    4
×   7
```

22)
```
    7
×   4
```
23)
```
    4
×   9
```
24)
```
    2
×   4
```
25)
```
    4
×   3
```
26)
```
    4
×   4
```
27)
```
    4
×   3
```
28)
```
   11
×   4
```

29)
```
    4
×   7
```
30)
```
    3
×   4
```
31)
```
    4
×   2
```
32)
```
    9
×   4
```
33)
```
    4
×   5
```
34)
```
   11
×   4
```
35)
```
    4
×  11
```

36)
```
    6
×   4
```
37)
```
    4
×   7
```
38)
```
    2
×   4
```
39)
```
    4
×   2
```
40)
```
    8
×   4
```
41)
```
    4
×   2
```
42)
```
    6
×   4
```

43)
```
    4
×   2
```
44)
```
    3
×   4
```
45)
```
    4
×  12
```
46)
```
   10
×   4
```
47)
```
    4
×   9
```
48)
```
    8
×   4
```
49)
```
    4
×   6
```

50)
```
    4
×   4
```
51)
```
    4
×   9
```
52)
```
    2
×   4
```
53)
```
    4
×   8
```
54)
```
    3
×   4
```
55)
```
    4
×   3
```
56)
```
    7
×   4
```

57)
```
    4
×   5
```
58)
```
    3
×   4
```
59)
```
    4
×  11
```
60)
```
   11
×   4
```

Time :

Score

/60

DAY 27
· Multiplying 4 ·

1)   4 × 9

2)   4 × 4

3)   4 × 6

4)   6 × 4

5)   4 × 2

6)   6 × 4

7)   4 × 8

8)   6 × 4

9)   4 × 9

10)   3 × 4

11)   4 × 5

12)   7 × 4

13)   4 × 8

14)   9 × 4

15)   4 × 3

16)   4 × 4

17)   4 × 8

18)   5 × 4

19)   4 × 3

20)   9 × 4

21)   4 × 8

22)   12 × 4

23)   4 × 9

24)   8 × 4

25)   4 × 7

26)   3 × 4

27)   4 × 10

28)   12 × 4

29)   4 × 10

30)   4 × 4

31)   4 × 12

32)   11 × 4

33)   4 × 9

34)   9 × 4

35)   4 × 2

36)   9 × 4

37)   4 × 10

38)   11 × 4

39)   4 × 6

40)   4 × 4

41)   4 × 12

42)   5 × 4

43)   4 × 6

44)   8 × 4

45)   4 × 6

46)   7 × 4

47)   4 × 2

48)   6 × 4

49)   4 × 3

50)   3 × 4

51)   4 × 7

52)   4 × 4

53)   4 × 9

54)   11 × 4

55)   4 × 6

56)   11 × 4

57)   4 × 5

58)   7 × 4

59)   4 × 6

60)   11 × 4

Time :

Score /60

HAVE YOU HEARD OF THALES OF MILETUS?

He is considered one of the earliest known mathematicians. He lived in Miletus, Ionia (now the area south of Izmir, Turkey) from 624-546 BC.

Using geometry, he was able to calculate the distance of ships from the shore as well as measure the heights of pyramids. His most notable contribution to mathematics is known as Thales Theorem, a proven theory in geometry used to this day!

DAY 28
· Multiplying 5 ·

1) $\begin{array}{r} 5 \\ \times\ 9 \\ \hline \end{array}$
2) $\begin{array}{r} 5 \\ \times\ 5 \\ \hline \end{array}$
3) $\begin{array}{r} 5 \\ \times\ 9 \\ \hline \end{array}$
4) $\begin{array}{r} 6 \\ \times\ 5 \\ \hline \end{array}$
5) $\begin{array}{r} 5 \\ \times\ 9 \\ \hline \end{array}$
6) $\begin{array}{r} 4 \\ \times\ 5 \\ \hline \end{array}$
7) $\begin{array}{r} 5 \\ \times\ 7 \\ \hline \end{array}$

8) $\begin{array}{r} 5 \\ \times\ 5 \\ \hline \end{array}$
9) $\begin{array}{r} 5 \\ \times\ 7 \\ \hline \end{array}$
10) $\begin{array}{r} 7 \\ \times\ 5 \\ \hline \end{array}$
11) $\begin{array}{r} 5 \\ \times\ 5 \\ \hline \end{array}$
12) $\begin{array}{r} 5 \\ \times\ 5 \\ \hline \end{array}$
13) $\begin{array}{r} 5 \\ \times\ 4 \\ \hline \end{array}$
14) $\begin{array}{r} 4 \\ \times\ 5 \\ \hline \end{array}$

15) $\begin{array}{r} 5 \\ \times\ 2 \\ \hline \end{array}$
16) $\begin{array}{r} 5 \\ \times\ 5 \\ \hline \end{array}$
17) $\begin{array}{r} 5 \\ \times\ 7 \\ \hline \end{array}$
18) $\begin{array}{r} 6 \\ \times\ 5 \\ \hline \end{array}$
19) $\begin{array}{r} 5 \\ \times\ 4 \\ \hline \end{array}$
20) $\begin{array}{r} 8 \\ \times\ 5 \\ \hline \end{array}$
21) $\begin{array}{r} 5 \\ \times\ 4 \\ \hline \end{array}$

22) $\begin{array}{r} 6 \\ \times\ 5 \\ \hline \end{array}$
23) $\begin{array}{r} 5 \\ \times\ 3 \\ \hline \end{array}$
24) $\begin{array}{r} 5 \\ \times\ 5 \\ \hline \end{array}$
25) $\begin{array}{r} 5 \\ \times\ 6 \\ \hline \end{array}$
26) $\begin{array}{r} 5 \\ \times\ 5 \\ \hline \end{array}$
27) $\begin{array}{r} 5 \\ \times\ 4 \\ \hline \end{array}$
28) $\begin{array}{r} 5 \\ \times\ 5 \\ \hline \end{array}$

29) $\begin{array}{r} 5 \\ \times\ 2 \\ \hline \end{array}$
30) $\begin{array}{r} 6 \\ \times\ 5 \\ \hline \end{array}$
31) $\begin{array}{r} 5 \\ \times\ 2 \\ \hline \end{array}$
32) $\begin{array}{r} 2 \\ \times\ 5 \\ \hline \end{array}$
33) $\begin{array}{r} 5 \\ \times\ 9 \\ \hline \end{array}$
34) $\begin{array}{r} 5 \\ \times\ 5 \\ \hline \end{array}$
35) $\begin{array}{r} 5 \\ \times\ 4 \\ \hline \end{array}$

36) $\begin{array}{r} 5 \\ \times\ 5 \\ \hline \end{array}$
37) $\begin{array}{r} 5 \\ \times\ 8 \\ \hline \end{array}$
38) $\begin{array}{r} 9 \\ \times\ 5 \\ \hline \end{array}$
39) $\begin{array}{r} 5 \\ \times\ 4 \\ \hline \end{array}$
40) $\begin{array}{r} 8 \\ \times\ 5 \\ \hline \end{array}$
41) $\begin{array}{r} 5 \\ \times\ 5 \\ \hline \end{array}$
42) $\begin{array}{r} 5 \\ \times\ 5 \\ \hline \end{array}$

43) $\begin{array}{r} 5 \\ \times\ 2 \\ \hline \end{array}$
44) $\begin{array}{r} 6 \\ \times\ 5 \\ \hline \end{array}$
45) $\begin{array}{r} 5 \\ \times\ 7 \\ \hline \end{array}$
46) $\begin{array}{r} 2 \\ \times\ 5 \\ \hline \end{array}$
47) $\begin{array}{r} 5 \\ \times\ 6 \\ \hline \end{array}$
48) $\begin{array}{r} 5 \\ \times\ 5 \\ \hline \end{array}$
49) $\begin{array}{r} 5 \\ \times\ 9 \\ \hline \end{array}$

50) $\begin{array}{r} 9 \\ \times\ 5 \\ \hline \end{array}$
51) $\begin{array}{r} 5 \\ \times\ 9 \\ \hline \end{array}$
52) $\begin{array}{r} 7 \\ \times\ 5 \\ \hline \end{array}$
53) $\begin{array}{r} 5 \\ \times\ 9 \\ \hline \end{array}$
54) $\begin{array}{r} 3 \\ \times\ 5 \\ \hline \end{array}$
55) $\begin{array}{r} 5 \\ \times\ 7 \\ \hline \end{array}$
56) $\begin{array}{r} 3 \\ \times\ 5 \\ \hline \end{array}$

57) $\begin{array}{r} 5 \\ \times\ 8 \\ \hline \end{array}$
58) $\begin{array}{r} 3 \\ \times\ 5 \\ \hline \end{array}$
59) $\begin{array}{r} 5 \\ \times\ 9 \\ \hline \end{array}$
60) $\begin{array}{r} 8 \\ \times\ 5 \\ \hline \end{array}$

Time :

Score /60

DAY 29
· Multiplying 5 ·

1) 5 × 4

2) 9 × 5

3) 5 × 8

4) 3 × 5

5) 5 × 6

6) 4 × 5

7) 5 × 8

8) 8 × 5

9) 5 × 3

10) 8 × 5

11) 5 × 6

12) 4 × 5

13) 5 × 6

14) 5 × 5

15) 5 × 2

16) 5 × 5

17) 5 × 3

18) 5 × 5

19) 5 × 3

20) 8 × 5

21) 5 × 9

22) 8 × 5

23) 5 × 8

24) 6 × 5

25) 5 × 3

26) 8 × 5

27) 5 × 7

28) 7 × 5

29) 5 × 7

30) 9 × 5

31) 5 × 7

32) 2 × 5

33) 5 × 9

34) 4 × 5

35) 5 × 6

36) 5 × 5

37) 5 × 5

38) 4 × 5

39) 5 × 5

40) 9 × 5

41) 5 × 9

42) 6 × 5

43) 5 × 5

44) 6 × 5

45) 5 × 3

46) 7 × 5

47) 5 × 9

48) 3 × 5

49) 5 × 6

50) 2 × 5

51) 5 × 7

52) 3 × 5

53) 5 × 5

54) 8 × 5

55) 5 × 6

56) 4 × 5

57) 5 × 5

58) 4 × 5

59) 5 × 8

60) 2 × 5

Time :

Score /60

DAY 30
· Multiplying 5 ·

1) 5 × 8

2) 5 × 5

3) 5 × 2

4) 0 × 5

5) 5 × 3

6) 5 × 5

7) 5 × 3

8) 2 × 5

9) 5 × 8

10) 8 × 5

11) 5 × 5

12) 8 × 5

13) 5 × 1

14) 8 × 5

15) 5 × 8

16) 3 × 5

17) 5 × 7

18) 5 × 5

19) 5 × 9

20) 7 × 5

21) 5 × 1

22) 3 × 5

23) 5 × 7

24) 5 × 5

25) 5 × 3

26) 8 × 5

27) 5 × 7

28) 2 × 5

29) 5 × 0

30) 1 × 5

31) 5 × 7

32) 6 × 5

33) 5 × 6

34) 7 × 5

35) 5 × 8

36) 3 × 5

37) 5 × 5

38) 5 × 5

39) 5 × 6

40) 6 × 5

41) 5 × 3

42) 9 × 5

43) 5 × 5

44) 2 × 5

45) 5 × 7

46) 8 × 5

47) 5 × 6

48) 5 × 5

49) 5 × 8

50) 3 × 5

51) 5 × 1

52) 0 × 5

53) 5 × 2

54) 7 × 5

55) 5 × 0

56) 6 × 5

57) 5 × 0

58) 4 × 5

59) 5 × 9

60) 4 × 5

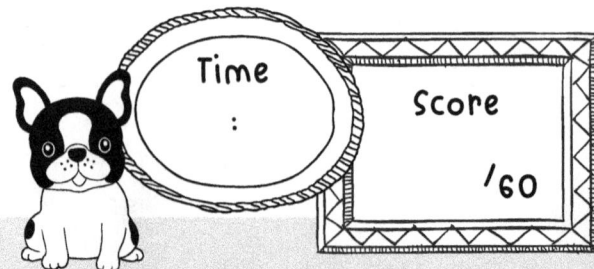

Time :

Score /60

DAY 31
· Multiplying 5 ·

1) $\begin{array}{r} 5 \\ \times\ 4 \\ \hline \end{array}$
2) $\begin{array}{r} 5 \\ \times\ 5 \\ \hline \end{array}$
3) $\begin{array}{r} 5 \\ \times\ 9 \\ \hline \end{array}$
4) $\begin{array}{r} 2 \\ \times\ 5 \\ \hline \end{array}$
5) $\begin{array}{r} 5 \\ \times\ 4 \\ \hline \end{array}$
6) $\begin{array}{r} 8 \\ \times\ 5 \\ \hline \end{array}$
7) $\begin{array}{r} 5 \\ \times\ 6 \\ \hline \end{array}$

8) $\begin{array}{r} 5 \\ \times\ 5 \\ \hline \end{array}$
9) $\begin{array}{r} 5 \\ \times\ 9 \\ \hline \end{array}$
10) $\begin{array}{r} 5 \\ \times\ 5 \\ \hline \end{array}$
11) $\begin{array}{r} 5 \\ \times\ 5 \\ \hline \end{array}$
12) $\begin{array}{r} 2 \\ \times\ 5 \\ \hline \end{array}$
13) $\begin{array}{r} 5 \\ \times\ 4 \\ \hline \end{array}$
14) $\begin{array}{r} 3 \\ \times\ 5 \\ \hline \end{array}$

15) $\begin{array}{r} 5 \\ \times\ 6 \\ \hline \end{array}$
16) $\begin{array}{r} 9 \\ \times\ 5 \\ \hline \end{array}$
17) $\begin{array}{r} 5 \\ \times\ 3 \\ \hline \end{array}$
18) $\begin{array}{r} 2 \\ \times\ 5 \\ \hline \end{array}$
19) $\begin{array}{r} 5 \\ \times\ 2 \\ \hline \end{array}$
20) $\begin{array}{r} 8 \\ \times\ 5 \\ \hline \end{array}$
21) $\begin{array}{r} 5 \\ \times\ 5 \\ \hline \end{array}$

22) $\begin{array}{r} 4 \\ \times\ 5 \\ \hline \end{array}$
23) $\begin{array}{r} 5 \\ \times\ 6 \\ \hline \end{array}$
24) $\begin{array}{r} 6 \\ \times\ 5 \\ \hline \end{array}$
25) $\begin{array}{r} 5 \\ \times\ 4 \\ \hline \end{array}$
26) $\begin{array}{r} 5 \\ \times\ 5 \\ \hline \end{array}$
27) $\begin{array}{r} 5 \\ \times\ 2 \\ \hline \end{array}$
28) $\begin{array}{r} 7 \\ \times\ 5 \\ \hline \end{array}$

29) $\begin{array}{r} 5 \\ \times\ 6 \\ \hline \end{array}$
30) $\begin{array}{r} 4 \\ \times\ 5 \\ \hline \end{array}$
31) $\begin{array}{r} 5 \\ \times\ 3 \\ \hline \end{array}$
32) $\begin{array}{r} 8 \\ \times\ 5 \\ \hline \end{array}$
33) $\begin{array}{r} 5 \\ \times\ 7 \\ \hline \end{array}$
34) $\begin{array}{r} 7 \\ \times\ 5 \\ \hline \end{array}$
35) $\begin{array}{r} 5 \\ \times\ 5 \\ \hline \end{array}$

36) $\begin{array}{r} 7 \\ \times\ 5 \\ \hline \end{array}$
37) $\begin{array}{r} 5 \\ \times\ 9 \\ \hline \end{array}$
38) $\begin{array}{r} 4 \\ \times\ 5 \\ \hline \end{array}$
39) $\begin{array}{r} 5 \\ \times\ 3 \\ \hline \end{array}$
40) $\begin{array}{r} 8 \\ \times\ 5 \\ \hline \end{array}$
41) $\begin{array}{r} 5 \\ \times\ 2 \\ \hline \end{array}$
42) $\begin{array}{r} 2 \\ \times\ 5 \\ \hline \end{array}$

43) $\begin{array}{r} 5 \\ \times\ 8 \\ \hline \end{array}$
44) $\begin{array}{r} 7 \\ \times\ 5 \\ \hline \end{array}$
45) $\begin{array}{r} 5 \\ \times\ 6 \\ \hline \end{array}$
46) $\begin{array}{r} 2 \\ \times\ 5 \\ \hline \end{array}$
47) $\begin{array}{r} 5 \\ \times\ 7 \\ \hline \end{array}$
48) $\begin{array}{r} 7 \\ \times\ 5 \\ \hline \end{array}$
49) $\begin{array}{r} 5 \\ \times\ 8 \\ \hline \end{array}$

50) $\begin{array}{r} 5 \\ \times\ 5 \\ \hline \end{array}$
51) $\begin{array}{r} 5 \\ \times\ 2 \\ \hline \end{array}$
52) $\begin{array}{r} 3 \\ \times\ 5 \\ \hline \end{array}$
53) $\begin{array}{r} 5 \\ \times\ 2 \\ \hline \end{array}$
54) $\begin{array}{r} 8 \\ \times\ 5 \\ \hline \end{array}$
55) $\begin{array}{r} 5 \\ \times\ 7 \\ \hline \end{array}$
56) $\begin{array}{r} 5 \\ \times\ 5 \\ \hline \end{array}$

57) $\begin{array}{r} 5 \\ \times\ 5 \\ \hline \end{array}$
58) $\begin{array}{r} 9 \\ \times\ 5 \\ \hline \end{array}$
59) $\begin{array}{r} 5 \\ \times\ 3 \\ \hline \end{array}$
60) $\begin{array}{r} 3 \\ \times\ 5 \\ \hline \end{array}$

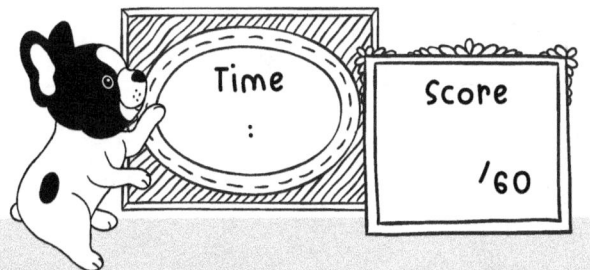

Time :

Score /60

DAY 32
· Multiplying 5 ·

1) 5 × 8

2) 12 × 5

3) 5 × 4

4) 10 × 5

5) 5 × 7

6) 9 × 5

7) 5 × 11

8) 2 × 5

9) 5 × 4

10) 6 × 5

11) 5 × 10

12) 8 × 5

13) 5 × 11

14) 9 × 5

15) 5 × 2

16) 2 × 5

17) 5 × 12

18) 2 × 5

19) 5 × 5

20) 5 × 5

21) 5 × 4

22) 8 × 5

23) 5 × 4

24) 12 × 5

25) 5 × 8

26) 6 × 5

27) 5 × 11

28) 5 × 5

29) 5 × 9

30) 7 × 5

31) 5 × 4

32) 6 × 5

33) 5 × 6

34) 4 × 5

35) 5 × 9

36) 2 × 5

37) 5 × 2

38) 9 × 5

39) 5 × 12

40) 8 × 5

41) 5 × 6

42) 10 × 5

43) 5 × 7

44) 7 × 5

45) 5 × 3

46) 3 × 5

47) 5 × 6

48) 4 × 5

49) 5 × 12

50) 9 × 5

51) 5 × 6

52) 6 × 5

53) 5 × 5

54) 10 × 5

55) 5 × 10

56) 11 × 5

57) 5 × 3

58) 2 × 5

59) 5 × 3

60) 5 × 5

Time :

Score /60

DAY 33

· Multiplying 5 ·

1)
$$\begin{array}{r} 5 \\ \times\ 7 \\ \hline \end{array}$$
2)
$$\begin{array}{r} 6 \\ \times\ 5 \\ \hline \end{array}$$
3)
$$\begin{array}{r} 5 \\ \times\ 9 \\ \hline \end{array}$$
4)
$$\begin{array}{r} 0 \\ \times\ 5 \\ \hline \end{array}$$
5)
$$\begin{array}{r} 5 \\ \times\ 4 \\ \hline \end{array}$$
6)
$$\begin{array}{r} 10 \\ \times\ 5 \\ \hline \end{array}$$
7)
$$\begin{array}{r} 5 \\ \times\ 0 \\ \hline \end{array}$$

8)
$$\begin{array}{r} 3 \\ \times\ 5 \\ \hline \end{array}$$
9)
$$\begin{array}{r} 5 \\ \times\ 2 \\ \hline \end{array}$$
10)
$$\begin{array}{r} 7 \\ \times\ 5 \\ \hline \end{array}$$
11)
$$\begin{array}{r} 5 \\ \times\ 10 \\ \hline \end{array}$$
12)
$$\begin{array}{r} 1 \\ \times\ 5 \\ \hline \end{array}$$
13)
$$\begin{array}{r} 5 \\ \times\ 11 \\ \hline \end{array}$$
14)
$$\begin{array}{r} 4 \\ \times\ 5 \\ \hline \end{array}$$

15)
$$\begin{array}{r} 5 \\ \times\ 2 \\ \hline \end{array}$$
16)
$$\begin{array}{r} 7 \\ \times\ 5 \\ \hline \end{array}$$
17)
$$\begin{array}{r} 5 \\ \times\ 6 \\ \hline \end{array}$$
18)
$$\begin{array}{r} 0 \\ \times\ 5 \\ \hline \end{array}$$
19)
$$\begin{array}{r} 5 \\ \times\ 11 \\ \hline \end{array}$$
20)
$$\begin{array}{r} 12 \\ \times\ 5 \\ \hline \end{array}$$
21)
$$\begin{array}{r} 5 \\ \times\ 1 \\ \hline \end{array}$$

22)
$$\begin{array}{r} 0 \\ \times\ 5 \\ \hline \end{array}$$
23)
$$\begin{array}{r} 5 \\ \times\ 11 \\ \hline \end{array}$$
24)
$$\begin{array}{r} 1 \\ \times\ 5 \\ \hline \end{array}$$
25)
$$\begin{array}{r} 5 \\ \times\ 11 \\ \hline \end{array}$$
26)
$$\begin{array}{r} 0 \\ \times\ 5 \\ \hline \end{array}$$
27)
$$\begin{array}{r} 5 \\ \times\ 11 \\ \hline \end{array}$$
28)
$$\begin{array}{r} 9 \\ \times\ 5 \\ \hline \end{array}$$

29)
$$\begin{array}{r} 5 \\ \times\ 8 \\ \hline \end{array}$$
30)
$$\begin{array}{r} 5 \\ \times\ 5 \\ \hline \end{array}$$
31)
$$\begin{array}{r} 5 \\ \times\ 0 \\ \hline \end{array}$$
32)
$$\begin{array}{r} 10 \\ \times\ 5 \\ \hline \end{array}$$
33)
$$\begin{array}{r} 5 \\ \times\ 3 \\ \hline \end{array}$$
34)
$$\begin{array}{r} 11 \\ \times\ 5 \\ \hline \end{array}$$
35)
$$\begin{array}{r} 5 \\ \times\ 12 \\ \hline \end{array}$$

36)
$$\begin{array}{r} 4 \\ \times\ 5 \\ \hline \end{array}$$
37)
$$\begin{array}{r} 5 \\ \times\ 3 \\ \hline \end{array}$$
38)
$$\begin{array}{r} 12 \\ \times\ 5 \\ \hline \end{array}$$
39)
$$\begin{array}{r} 5 \\ \times\ 3 \\ \hline \end{array}$$
40)
$$\begin{array}{r} 3 \\ \times\ 5 \\ \hline \end{array}$$
41)
$$\begin{array}{r} 5 \\ \times\ 9 \\ \hline \end{array}$$
42)
$$\begin{array}{r} 5 \\ \times\ 5 \\ \hline \end{array}$$

43)
$$\begin{array}{r} 5 \\ \times\ 0 \\ \hline \end{array}$$
44)
$$\begin{array}{r} 10 \\ \times\ 5 \\ \hline \end{array}$$
45)
$$\begin{array}{r} 5 \\ \times\ 7 \\ \hline \end{array}$$
46)
$$\begin{array}{r} 11 \\ \times\ 5 \\ \hline \end{array}$$
47)
$$\begin{array}{r} 5 \\ \times\ 2 \\ \hline \end{array}$$
48)
$$\begin{array}{r} 12 \\ \times\ 5 \\ \hline \end{array}$$
49)
$$\begin{array}{r} 5 \\ \times\ 7 \\ \hline \end{array}$$

50)
$$\begin{array}{r} 9 \\ \times\ 5 \\ \hline \end{array}$$
51)
$$\begin{array}{r} 5 \\ \times\ 8 \\ \hline \end{array}$$
52)
$$\begin{array}{r} 2 \\ \times\ 5 \\ \hline \end{array}$$
53)
$$\begin{array}{r} 5 \\ \times\ 9 \\ \hline \end{array}$$
54)
$$\begin{array}{r} 6 \\ \times\ 5 \\ \hline \end{array}$$
55)
$$\begin{array}{r} 5 \\ \times\ 7 \\ \hline \end{array}$$
56)
$$\begin{array}{r} 10 \\ \times\ 5 \\ \hline \end{array}$$

57)
$$\begin{array}{r} 5 \\ \times\ 5 \\ \hline \end{array}$$
58)
$$\begin{array}{r} 5 \\ \times\ 5 \\ \hline \end{array}$$
59)
$$\begin{array}{r} 5 \\ \times\ 3 \\ \hline \end{array}$$
60)
$$\begin{array}{r} 3 \\ \times\ 5 \\ \hline \end{array}$$

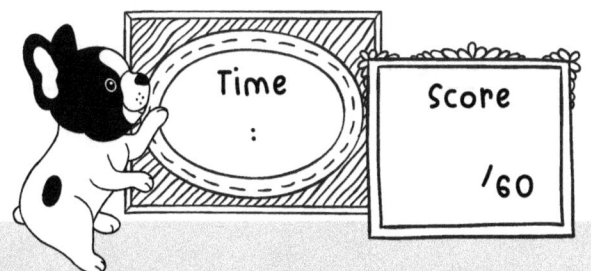

Time :

Score /60

DAY 34

· Multiplying 5 ·

1) 5 × 7

2) 8 × 5

3) 5 × 3

4) 8 × 5

5) 5 × 4

6) 4 × 5

7) 5 × 5

8) 6 × 5

9) 5 × 4

10) 11 × 5

11) 5 × 7

12) 9 × 5

13) 5 × 2

14) 9 × 5

15) 5 × 5

16) 12 × 5

17) 5 × 12

18) 2 × 5

19) 5 × 6

20) 2 × 5

21) 5 × 2

22) 2 × 5

23) 5 × 5

24) 4 × 5

25) 5 × 3

26) 3 × 5

27) 5 × 2

28) 8 × 5

29) 5 × 5

30) 11 × 5

31) 5 × 9

32) 6 × 5

33) 5 × 2

34) 10 × 5

35) 5 × 11

36) 3 × 5

37) 5 × 9

38) 2 × 5

39) 5 × 5

40) 8 × 5

41) 5 × 12

42) 9 × 5

43) 5 × 4

44) 6 × 5

45) 5 × 4

46) 5 × 5

47) 5 × 9

48) 11 × 5

49) 5 × 4

50) 10 × 5

51) 5 × 7

52) 8 × 5

53) 5 × 6

54) 5 × 5

55) 5 × 3

56) 2 × 5

57) 5 × 10

58) 5 × 5

59) 5 × 11

60) 12 × 5

Time :

Score /60

DAY 35
· Multiplying 5 ·

1) 5 × 4

2) 7 × 5

3) 5 × 4

4) 9 × 5

5) 5 × 12

6) 2 × 5

7) 5 × 3

8) 2 × 5

9) 5 × 12

10) 5 × 5

11) 5 × 12

12) 11 × 5

13) 5 × 4

14) 10 × 5

15) 5 × 2

16) 8 × 5

17) 5 × 7

18) 8 × 5

19) 5 × 3

20) 10 × 5

21) 5 × 6

22) 7 × 5

23) 5 × 4

24) 4 × 5

25) 5 × 4

26) 11 × 5

27) 5 × 8

28) 4 × 5

29) 5 × 9

30) 3 × 5

31) 5 × 5

32) 5 × 5

33) 5 × 5

34) 3 × 5

35) 5 × 4

36) 12 × 5

37) 5 × 12

38) 10 × 5

39) 5 × 10

40) 4 × 5

41) 5 × 11

42) 10 × 5

43) 5 × 11

44) 5 × 5

45) 5 × 12

46) 8 × 5

47) 5 × 5

48) 2 × 5

49) 5 × 3

50) 7 × 5

51) 5 × 11

52) 2 × 5

53) 5 × 2

54) 2 × 5

55) 5 × 11

56) 6 × 5

57) 5 × 5

58) 10 × 5

59) 5 × 6

60) 11 × 5

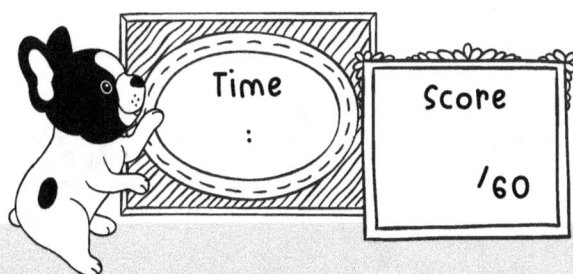

Time
:

Score
/60

THE RESULT OF
(6 X 9) + (6 + 9) = 69

This one actually works with any number as long as the 9 stays where it is!

For example: (73 x 9) + (73 + 9) = 739

Try putting another number in the place of 73 and see what you get!

DAY 36
· Multiplying 6 ·

1) $\begin{array}{r} 6 \\ \times\ 8 \\ \hline \end{array}$
2) $\begin{array}{r} 3 \\ \times\ 6 \\ \hline \end{array}$
3) $\begin{array}{r} 6 \\ \times\ 6 \\ \hline \end{array}$
4) $\begin{array}{r} 5 \\ \times\ 6 \\ \hline \end{array}$
5) $\begin{array}{r} 6 \\ \times\ 6 \\ \hline \end{array}$
6) $\begin{array}{r} 7 \\ \times\ 6 \\ \hline \end{array}$
7) $\begin{array}{r} 6 \\ \times\ 9 \\ \hline \end{array}$

8) $\begin{array}{r} 6 \\ \times\ 6 \\ \hline \end{array}$
9) $\begin{array}{r} 6 \\ \times\ 2 \\ \hline \end{array}$
10) $\begin{array}{r} 5 \\ \times\ 6 \\ \hline \end{array}$
11) $\begin{array}{r} 6 \\ \times\ 4 \\ \hline \end{array}$
12) $\begin{array}{r} 4 \\ \times\ 6 \\ \hline \end{array}$
13) $\begin{array}{r} 6 \\ \times\ 6 \\ \hline \end{array}$
14) $\begin{array}{r} 7 \\ \times\ 6 \\ \hline \end{array}$

15) $\begin{array}{r} 6 \\ \times\ 5 \\ \hline \end{array}$
16) $\begin{array}{r} 5 \\ \times\ 6 \\ \hline \end{array}$
17) $\begin{array}{r} 6 \\ \times\ 9 \\ \hline \end{array}$
18) $\begin{array}{r} 4 \\ \times\ 6 \\ \hline \end{array}$
19) $\begin{array}{r} 6 \\ \times\ 8 \\ \hline \end{array}$
20) $\begin{array}{r} 5 \\ \times\ 6 \\ \hline \end{array}$
21) $\begin{array}{r} 6 \\ \times\ 7 \\ \hline \end{array}$

22) $\begin{array}{r} 6 \\ \times\ 6 \\ \hline \end{array}$
23) $\begin{array}{r} 6 \\ \times\ 9 \\ \hline \end{array}$
24) $\begin{array}{r} 3 \\ \times\ 6 \\ \hline \end{array}$
25) $\begin{array}{r} 6 \\ \times\ 8 \\ \hline \end{array}$
26) $\begin{array}{r} 6 \\ \times\ 6 \\ \hline \end{array}$
27) $\begin{array}{r} 6 \\ \times\ 6 \\ \hline \end{array}$
28) $\begin{array}{r} 2 \\ \times\ 6 \\ \hline \end{array}$

29) $\begin{array}{r} 6 \\ \times\ 4 \\ \hline \end{array}$
30) $\begin{array}{r} 6 \\ \times\ 6 \\ \hline \end{array}$
31) $\begin{array}{r} 6 \\ \times\ 9 \\ \hline \end{array}$
32) $\begin{array}{r} 7 \\ \times\ 6 \\ \hline \end{array}$
33) $\begin{array}{r} 6 \\ \times\ 3 \\ \hline \end{array}$
34) $\begin{array}{r} 5 \\ \times\ 6 \\ \hline \end{array}$
35) $\begin{array}{r} 6 \\ \times\ 7 \\ \hline \end{array}$

36) $\begin{array}{r} 8 \\ \times\ 6 \\ \hline \end{array}$
37) $\begin{array}{r} 6 \\ \times\ 7 \\ \hline \end{array}$
38) $\begin{array}{r} 6 \\ \times\ 6 \\ \hline \end{array}$
39) $\begin{array}{r} 6 \\ \times\ 6 \\ \hline \end{array}$
40) $\begin{array}{r} 5 \\ \times\ 6 \\ \hline \end{array}$
41) $\begin{array}{r} 6 \\ \times\ 6 \\ \hline \end{array}$
42) $\begin{array}{r} 2 \\ \times\ 6 \\ \hline \end{array}$

43) $\begin{array}{r} 6 \\ \times\ 9 \\ \hline \end{array}$
44) $\begin{array}{r} 7 \\ \times\ 6 \\ \hline \end{array}$
45) $\begin{array}{r} 6 \\ \times\ 8 \\ \hline \end{array}$
46) $\begin{array}{r} 4 \\ \times\ 6 \\ \hline \end{array}$
47) $\begin{array}{r} 6 \\ \times\ 5 \\ \hline \end{array}$
48) $\begin{array}{r} 4 \\ \times\ 6 \\ \hline \end{array}$
49) $\begin{array}{r} 6 \\ \times\ 6 \\ \hline \end{array}$

50) $\begin{array}{r} 3 \\ \times\ 6 \\ \hline \end{array}$
51) $\begin{array}{r} 6 \\ \times\ 8 \\ \hline \end{array}$
52) $\begin{array}{r} 4 \\ \times\ 6 \\ \hline \end{array}$
53) $\begin{array}{r} 6 \\ \times\ 2 \\ \hline \end{array}$
54) $\begin{array}{r} 6 \\ \times\ 6 \\ \hline \end{array}$
55) $\begin{array}{r} 6 \\ \times\ 5 \\ \hline \end{array}$
56) $\begin{array}{r} 2 \\ \times\ 6 \\ \hline \end{array}$

57) $\begin{array}{r} 6 \\ \times\ 5 \\ \hline \end{array}$
58) $\begin{array}{r} 2 \\ \times\ 6 \\ \hline \end{array}$
59) $\begin{array}{r} 6 \\ \times\ 6 \\ \hline \end{array}$
60) $\begin{array}{r} 2 \\ \times\ 6 \\ \hline \end{array}$

Time :

Score

/60

DAY 37

· Multiplying 6 ·

1) 6 × 0

2) 5 × 6

3) 6 × 0

4) 3 × 6

5) 6 × 3

6) 6 × 6

7) 6 × 1

8) 6 × 6

9) 6 × 8

10) 1 × 6

11) 6 × 7

12) 0 × 6

13) 6 × 9

14) 5 × 6

15) 6 × 2

16) 8 × 6

17) 6 × 2

18) 7 × 6

19) 6 × 9

20) 6 × 6

21) 6 × 6

22) 7 × 6

23) 6 × 3

24) 6 × 6

25) 6 × 8

26) 9 × 6

27) 6 × 4

28) 5 × 6

29) 6 × 9

30) 5 × 6

31) 6 × 1

32) 8 × 6

33) 6 × 1

34) 3 × 6

35) 6 × 1

36) 4 × 6

37) 6 × 6

38) 2 × 6

39) 6 × 7

40) 6 × 6

41) 6 × 7

42) 6 × 6

43) 6 × 6

44) 3 × 6

45) 6 × 0

46) 2 × 6

47) 6 × 5

48) 5 × 6

49) 6 × 1

50) 9 × 6

51) 6 × 4

52) 0 × 6

53) 6 × 5

54) 7 × 6

55) 6 × 1

56) 3 × 6

57) 6 × 1

58) 8 × 6

59) 6 × 0

60) 7 × 6

Time :

Score /60

DAY 38
· Multiplying 6 ·

1) 6 × 9

2) 6 × 6

3) 6 × 3

4) 5 × 6

5) 6 × 5

6) 4 × 6

7) 6 × 5

8) 2 × 6

9) 6 × 8

10) 2 × 6

11) 6 × 3

12) 2 × 6

13) 6 × 2

14) 5 × 6

15) 6 × 5

16) 7 × 6

17) 6 × 6

18) 7 × 6

19) 6 × 2

20) 5 × 6

21) 6 × 3

22) 5 × 6

23) 6 × 6

24) 4 × 6

25) 6 × 7

26) 5 × 6

27) 6 × 2

28) 4 × 6

29) 6 × 2

30) 3 × 6

31) 6 × 8

32) 4 × 6

33) 6 × 6

34) 8 × 6

35) 6 × 5

36) 3 × 6

37) 6 × 6

38) 4 × 6

39) 6 × 2

40) 7 × 6

41) 6 × 4

42) 6 × 6

43) 6 × 9

44) 3 × 6

45) 6 × 9

46) 7 × 6

47) 6 × 9

48) 7 × 6

49) 6 × 2

50) 4 × 6

51) 6 × 9

52) 9 × 6

53) 6 × 3

54) 2 × 6

55) 6 × 9

56) 3 × 6

57) 6 × 7

58) 8 × 6

59) 6 × 4

60) 5 × 6

Time :

Score /60

DAY 39
· Multiplying 6 ·

1) 6 × 6

2) 2 × 6

3) 6 × 8

4) 7 × 6

5) 6 × 9

6) 5 × 6

7) 6 × 9

8) 6 × 6

9) 6 × 3

10) 5 × 6

11) 6 × 6

12) 9 × 6

13) 6 × 9

14) 9 × 6

15) 6 × 8

16) 7 × 6

17) 6 × 8

18) 7 × 6

19) 6 × 4

20) 2 × 6

21) 6 × 8

22) 6 × 6

23) 6 × 8

24) 8 × 6

25) 6 × 8

26) 2 × 6

27) 6 × 9

28) 5 × 6

29) 6 × 6

30) 8 × 6

31) 6 × 3

32) 3 × 6

33) 6 × 9

34) 5 × 6

35) 6 × 6

36) 2 × 6

37) 6 × 7

38) 4 × 6

39) 6 × 4

40) 6 × 6

41) 6 × 6

42) 9 × 6

43) 6 × 8

44) 8 × 6

45) 6 × 4

46) 3 × 6

47) 6 × 3

48) 3 × 6

49) 6 × 4

50) 2 × 6

51) 6 × 9

52) 8 × 6

53) 6 × 9

54) 9 × 6

55) 6 × 2

56) 7 × 6

57) 6 × 5

58) 8 × 6

59) 6 × 3

60) 2 × 6

Time :

Score /60

DAY 40

· Multiplying 6 ·

1) 6 × 3

2) 2 × 6

3) 6 × 11

4) 2 × 6

5) 6 × 12

6) 9 × 6

7) 6 × 7

8) 9 × 6

9) 6 × 9

10) 8 × 6

11) 6 × 10

12) 7 × 6

13) 6 × 8

14) 4 × 6

15) 6 × 5

16) 11 × 6

17) 6 × 5

18) 5 × 6

19) 6 × 12

20) 9 × 6

21) 6 × 7

22) 8 × 6

23) 6 × 7

24) 5 × 6

25) 6 × 3

26) 5 × 6

27) 6 × 3

28) 6 × 6

29) 6 × 2

30) 11 × 6

31) 6 × 3

32) 7 × 6

33) 6 × 8

34) 2 × 6

35) 6 × 11

36) 5 × 6

37) 6 × 7

38) 9 × 6

39) 6 × 3

40) 11 × 6

41) 6 × 8

42) 2 × 6

43) 6 × 10

44) 6 × 6

45) 6 × 6

46) 4 × 6

47) 6 × 4

48) 5 × 6

49) 6 × 5

50) 10 × 6

51) 6 × 7

52) 11 × 6

53) 6 × 3

54) 4 × 6

55) 6 × 8

56) 4 × 6

57) 6 × 4

58) 9 × 6

59) 6 × 7

60) 3 × 6

Time :

Score /60

DAY 41
· Multiplying 6 ·

1)
```
    6
×   5
```

2)
```
    4
×   6
```

3)
```
    6
×   6
```

4)
```
    4
×   6
```

5)
```
     6
×   12
```

6)
```
   11
×   6
```

7)
```
    6
×   6
```

8)
```
    8
×   6
```

9)
```
     6
×   11
```

10)
```
    4
×   6
```

11)
```
    6
×   8
```

12)
```
   11
×   6
```

13)
```
    6
×   8
```

14)
```
    7
×   6
```

15)
```
    6
×   7
```

16)
```
    5
×   6
```

17)
```
    6
×   3
```

18)
```
   11
×   6
```

19)
```
    6
×   6
```

20)
```
    4
×   6
```

21)
```
    6
×   8
```

22)
```
    8
×   6
```

23)
```
    6
×   5
```

24)
```
   10
×   6
```

25)
```
    6
×   2
```

26)
```
    9
×   6
```

27)
```
     6
×   12
```

28)
```
    4
×   6
```

29)
```
    6
×   3
```

30)
```
    3
×   6
```

31)
```
    6
×   9
```

32)
```
    6
×   6
```

33)
```
    6
×   11
```

34)
```
    8
×   6
```

35)
```
    6
×   4
```

36)
```
    6
×   6
```

37)
```
    6
×   9
```

38)
```
   12
×   6
```

39)
```
    6
×   9
```

40)
```
   11
×   6
```

41)
```
    6
×   11
```

42)
```
    5
×   6
```

43)
```
    6
×   12
```

44)
```
   12
×   6
```

45)
```
    6
×   5
```

46)
```
    8
×   6
```

47)
```
    6
×   6
```

48)
```
   11
×   6
```

49)
```
    6
×   6
```

50)
```
    3
×   6
```

51)
```
    6
×   7
```

52)
```
    3
×   6
```

53)
```
    6
×   6
```

54)
```
    3
×   6
```

55)
```
    6
×   10
```

56)
```
    5
×   6
```

57)
```
    6
×   5
```

58)
```
    6
×   6
```

59)
```
    6
×   4
```

60)
```
   12
×   6
```

Time :

Score /60

DAY 42
· Multiplying 6 ·

1) 6 × 0

2) 4 × 6

3) 6 × 1

4) 7 × 6

5) 6 × 5

6) 0 × 6

7) 6 × 1

8) 5 × 6

9) 6 × 12

10) 3 × 6

11) 6 × 6

12) 12 × 6

13) 6 × 1

14) 2 × 6

15) 6 × 1

16) 11 × 6

17) 6 × 8

18) 5 × 6

19) 6 × 2

20) 0 × 6

21) 6 × 12

22) 9 × 6

23) 6 × 3

24) 12 × 6

25) 6 × 4

26) 3 × 6

27) 6 × 0

28) 4 × 6

29) 6 × 1

30) 8 × 6

31) 6 × 2

32) 0 × 6

33) 6 × 0

34) 8 × 6

35) 6 × 1

36) 10 × 6

37) 6 × 1

38) 6 × 6

39) 6 × 1

40) 9 × 6

41) 6 × 5

42) 11 × 6

43) 6 × 3

44) 3 × 6

45) 6 × 3

46) 11 × 6

47) 6 × 12

48) 5 × 6

49) 6 × 3

50) 6 × 6

51) 6 × 12

52) 3 × 6

53) 6 × 2

54) 6 × 6

55) 6 × 7

56) 9 × 6

57) 6 × 1

58) 6 × 6

59) 6 × 8

60) 10 × 6

Time :

Score /60

DAY 43

· Multiplying 6 ·

1) 6 × 5
2) 10 × 6
3) 6 × 9
4) 3 × 6
5) 6 × 12
6) 5 × 6
7) 6 × 2

8) 10 × 6
9) 6 × 12
10) 12 × 6
11) 6 × 6
12) 9 × 6
13) 6 × 8
14) 7 × 6

15) 6 × 12
16) 8 × 6
17) 6 × 12
18) 3 × 6
19) 6 × 9
20) 4 × 6
21) 6 × 4

22) 9 × 6
23) 6 × 5
24) 2 × 6
25) 6 × 2
26) 2 × 6
27) 6 × 10
28) 5 × 6

29) 6 × 5
30) 6 × 6
31) 6 × 2
32) 6 × 6
33) 6 × 9
34) 10 × 6
35) 6 × 2

36) 8 × 6
37) 6 × 6
38) 11 × 6
39) 6 × 4
40) 10 × 6
41) 6 × 9
42) 11 × 6

43) 6 × 3
44) 10 × 6
45) 6 × 3
46) 4 × 6
47) 6 × 12
48) 2 × 6
49) 6 × 5

50) 4 × 6
51) 6 × 11
52) 2 × 6
53) 6 × 11
54) 2 × 6
55) 6 × 5
56) 11 × 6

57) 6 × 5
58) 8 × 6
59) 6 × 7
60) 6 × 6

Time :

Score /60

DID YOU KNOW THAT EVERY SINGLE ODD NUMBER IS SPELLED WITH AN 'E'?

One, three, five, seven, nine, eleven!

Even when you use larger numbers that are odd, they will still include one, three, five, seven, or nine.

For example: Four hundred and eighty-three!

DAY 44
· Multiplying 7 ·

1) 7 × 8

2) 9 × 7

3) 7 × 3

4) 3 × 7

5) 7 × 6

6) 9 × 7

7) 7 × 8

8) 3 × 7

9) 7 × 6

10) 7 × 0

11) 7 × 7

12) 2 × 7

13) 7 × 8

14) 7 × 4

15) 7 × 3

16) 3 × 7

17) 7 × 8

18) 3 × 7

19) 7 × 6

20) 7 × 7

21) 7 × 8

22) 4 × 7

23) 7 × 2

24) 8 × 7

25) 7 × 2

26) 7 × 6

27) 7 × 7

28) 6 × 7

29) 7 × 2

30) 7 × 7

31) 7 × 0

32) 9 × 7

33) 7 × 7

34) 8 × 7

35) 7 × 2

36) 5 × 7

37) 7 × 4

38) 9 × 7

39) 7 × 2

40) 4 × 7

41) 7 × 3

42) 9 × 7

43) 7 × 4

44) 2 × 7

45) 7 × 4

46) 3 × 7

47) 7 × 5

48) 3 × 7

49) 7 × 2

50) 7 × 2

51) 7 × 9

52) 3 × 7

53) 7 × 1

54) 8 × 7

55) 7 × 8

56) 7 × 7

57) 7 × 2

58) 7 × 7

59) 7 × 6

60) 5 × 7

Time :

Score /60

DAY 45

· Multiplying 7 ·

1) 7 × 8

2) 4 × 7

3) 7 × 9

4) 7 × 7

5) 7 × 6

6) 9 × 7

7) 7 × 5

8) 9 × 7

9) 7 × 3

10) 9 × 7

11) 7 × 8

12) 3 × 7

13) 7 × 6

14) 2 × 7

15) 7 × 7

16) 6 × 7

17) 7 × 3

18) 4 × 7

19) 7 × 8

20) 8 × 7

21) 7 × 2

22) 5 × 7

23) 7 × 7

24) 3 × 7

25) 7 × 9

26) 6 × 7

27) 7 × 7

28) 4 × 7

29) 7 × 6

30) 4 × 7

31) 7 × 6

32) 8 × 7

33) 7 × 3

34) 7 × 7

35) 7 × 8

36) 9 × 7

37) 7 × 3

38) 2 × 7

39) 7 × 4

40) 6 × 7

41) 7 × 2

42) 2 × 7

43) 7 × 6

44) 2 × 7

45) 7 × 5

46) 9 × 7

47) 7 × 9

48) 3 × 7

49) 7 × 3

50) 4 × 7

51) 7 × 3

52) 6 × 7

53) 7 × 6

54) 8 × 7

55) 7 × 8

56) 8 × 7

57) 7 × 8

58) 7 × 7

59) 7 × 4

60) 7 × 7

Time :

Score /60

DAY 46
· Multiplying 7 ·

1) 7
  × 9

2) 7
  × 7

3) 7
  × 3

4) 3
  × 7

5) 7
  × 6

6) 3
  × 7

7) 7
  × 3

8) 4
  × 7

9) 7
  × 0

10) 0
   × 7

11) 7
   × 2

12) 6
   × 7

13) 7
   × 8

14) 4
   × 7

15) 7
   × 4

16) 0
   × 7

17) 7
   × 5

18) 5
   × 7

19) 7
   × 0

20) 4
   × 7

21) 7
   × 4

22) 5
   × 7

23) 7
   × 2

24) 7
   × 7

25) 7
   × 1

26) 1
   × 7

27) 7
   × 3

28) 1
   × 7

29) 7
   × 2

30) 6
   × 7

31) 7
   × 2

32) 9
   × 7

33) 7
   × 0

34) 9
   × 7

35) 7
   × 5

36) 8
   × 7

37) 7
   × 9

38) 7
   × 7

39) 7
   × 4

40) 0
   × 7

41) 7
   × 3

42) 5
   × 7

43) 7
   × 4

44) 3
   × 7

45) 7
   × 4

46) 7
   × 7

47) 7
   × 0

48) 6
   × 7

49) 7
   × 5

50) 2
   × 7

51) 7
   × 3

52) 5
   × 7

53) 7
   × 6

54) 9
   × 7

55) 7
   × 5

56) 6
   × 7

57) 7
   × 2

58) 8
   × 7

59) 7
   × 8

60) 3
   × 7

Time :

Score   /60

DAY 47
· Multiplying 7 ·

1) $\begin{array}{r} 7 \\ \times\ 3 \\ \hline \end{array}$
2) $\begin{array}{r} 3 \\ \times\ 7 \\ \hline \end{array}$
3) $\begin{array}{r} 7 \\ \times\ 4 \\ \hline \end{array}$
4) $\begin{array}{r} 3 \\ \times\ 7 \\ \hline \end{array}$
5) $\begin{array}{r} 7 \\ \times\ 6 \\ \hline \end{array}$
6) $\begin{array}{r} 6 \\ \times\ 7 \\ \hline \end{array}$
7) $\begin{array}{r} 7 \\ \times\ 7 \\ \hline \end{array}$

8) $\begin{array}{r} 9 \\ \times\ 7 \\ \hline \end{array}$
9) $\begin{array}{r} 7 \\ \times\ 3 \\ \hline \end{array}$
10) $\begin{array}{r} 4 \\ \times\ 7 \\ \hline \end{array}$
11) $\begin{array}{r} 7 \\ \times\ 9 \\ \hline \end{array}$
12) $\begin{array}{r} 5 \\ \times\ 7 \\ \hline \end{array}$
13) $\begin{array}{r} 7 \\ \times\ 8 \\ \hline \end{array}$
14) $\begin{array}{r} 8 \\ \times\ 7 \\ \hline \end{array}$

15) $\begin{array}{r} 7 \\ \times\ 9 \\ \hline \end{array}$
16) $\begin{array}{r} 5 \\ \times\ 7 \\ \hline \end{array}$
17) $\begin{array}{r} 7 \\ \times\ 7 \\ \hline \end{array}$
18) $\begin{array}{r} 5 \\ \times\ 7 \\ \hline \end{array}$
19) $\begin{array}{r} 7 \\ \times\ 3 \\ \hline \end{array}$
20) $\begin{array}{r} 5 \\ \times\ 7 \\ \hline \end{array}$
21) $\begin{array}{r} 7 \\ \times\ 7 \\ \hline \end{array}$

22) $\begin{array}{r} 2 \\ \times\ 7 \\ \hline \end{array}$
23) $\begin{array}{r} 7 \\ \times\ 5 \\ \hline \end{array}$
24) $\begin{array}{r} 8 \\ \times\ 7 \\ \hline \end{array}$
25) $\begin{array}{r} 7 \\ \times\ 3 \\ \hline \end{array}$
26) $\begin{array}{r} 2 \\ \times\ 7 \\ \hline \end{array}$
27) $\begin{array}{r} 7 \\ \times\ 7 \\ \hline \end{array}$
28) $\begin{array}{r} 3 \\ \times\ 7 \\ \hline \end{array}$

29) $\begin{array}{r} 7 \\ \times\ 8 \\ \hline \end{array}$
30) $\begin{array}{r} 7 \\ \times\ 7 \\ \hline \end{array}$
31) $\begin{array}{r} 7 \\ \times\ 8 \\ \hline \end{array}$
32) $\begin{array}{r} 4 \\ \times\ 7 \\ \hline \end{array}$
33) $\begin{array}{r} 7 \\ \times\ 9 \\ \hline \end{array}$
34) $\begin{array}{r} 9 \\ \times\ 7 \\ \hline \end{array}$
35) $\begin{array}{r} 7 \\ \times\ 4 \\ \hline \end{array}$

36) $\begin{array}{r} 6 \\ \times\ 7 \\ \hline \end{array}$
37) $\begin{array}{r} 7 \\ \times\ 3 \\ \hline \end{array}$
38) $\begin{array}{r} 8 \\ \times\ 7 \\ \hline \end{array}$
39) $\begin{array}{r} 7 \\ \times\ 4 \\ \hline \end{array}$
40) $\begin{array}{r} 2 \\ \times\ 7 \\ \hline \end{array}$
41) $\begin{array}{r} 7 \\ \times\ 7 \\ \hline \end{array}$
42) $\begin{array}{r} 5 \\ \times\ 7 \\ \hline \end{array}$

43) $\begin{array}{r} 7 \\ \times\ 3 \\ \hline \end{array}$
44) $\begin{array}{r} 7 \\ \times\ 7 \\ \hline \end{array}$
45) $\begin{array}{r} 7 \\ \times\ 9 \\ \hline \end{array}$
46) $\begin{array}{r} 4 \\ \times\ 7 \\ \hline \end{array}$
47) $\begin{array}{r} 7 \\ \times\ 6 \\ \hline \end{array}$
48) $\begin{array}{r} 4 \\ \times\ 7 \\ \hline \end{array}$
49) $\begin{array}{r} 7 \\ \times\ 5 \\ \hline \end{array}$

50) $\begin{array}{r} 5 \\ \times\ 7 \\ \hline \end{array}$
51) $\begin{array}{r} 7 \\ \times\ 9 \\ \hline \end{array}$
52) $\begin{array}{r} 4 \\ \times\ 7 \\ \hline \end{array}$
53) $\begin{array}{r} 7 \\ \times\ 9 \\ \hline \end{array}$
54) $\begin{array}{r} 8 \\ \times\ 7 \\ \hline \end{array}$
55) $\begin{array}{r} 7 \\ \times\ 6 \\ \hline \end{array}$
56) $\begin{array}{r} 9 \\ \times\ 7 \\ \hline \end{array}$

57) $\begin{array}{r} 7 \\ \times\ 2 \\ \hline \end{array}$
58) $\begin{array}{r} 4 \\ \times\ 7 \\ \hline \end{array}$
59) $\begin{array}{r} 7 \\ \times\ 4 \\ \hline \end{array}$
60) $\begin{array}{r} 8 \\ \times\ 7 \\ \hline \end{array}$

Time
:

Score
/60

DAY 48
· Multiplying 7 ·

1) 7 × 6

2) 10 × 7

3) 7 × 3

4) 2 × 7

5) 7 × 10

6) 8 × 7

7) 7 × 8

8) 8 × 7

9) 7 × 11

10) 11 × 7

11) 7 × 3

12) 8 × 7

13) 7 × 11

14) 6 × 7

15) 7 × 9

16) 2 × 7

17) 7 × 3

18) 10 × 7

19) 7 × 3

20) 3 × 7

21) 7 × 4

22) 2 × 7

23) 7 × 8

24) 3 × 7

25) 7 × 6

26) 10 × 7

27) 7 × 5

28) 5 × 7

29) 7 × 4

30) 8 × 7

31) 7 × 9

32) 8 × 7

33) 7 × 7

34) 11 × 7

35) 7 × 6

36) 10 × 7

37) 7 × 7

38) 10 × 7

39) 7 × 8

40) 2 × 7

41) 7 × 12

42) 8 × 7

43) 7 × 2

44) 12 × 7

45) 7 × 10

46) 8 × 7

47) 7 × 9

48) 9 × 7

49) 7 × 4

50) 7 × 7

51) 7 × 7

52) 9 × 7

53) 7 × 8

54) 5 × 7

55) 7 × 8

56) 6 × 7

57) 7 × 8

58) 8 × 7

59) 7 × 6

60) 12 × 7

Time

:

Score

/60

DAY 49
· Multiplying 7 ·

1) 7 × 4
2) 9 × 7
3) 7 × 8
4) 8 × 7
5) 7 × 6
6) 2 × 7
7) 7 × 8

8) 12 × 7
9) 7 × 7
10) 3 × 7
11) 7 × 10
12) 10 × 7
13) 7 × 3
14) 9 × 7

15) 7 × 10
16) 2 × 7
17) 7 × 7
18) 8 × 7
19) 7 × 11
20) 12 × 7
21) 7 × 11

22) 7 × 7
23) 7 × 12
24) 12 × 7
25) 7 × 3
26) 6 × 7
27) 7 × 10
28) 5 × 7

29) 7 × 11
30) 8 × 7
31) 7 × 7
32) 9 × 7
33) 7 × 3
34) 10 × 7
35) 7 × 2

36) 3 × 7
37) 7 × 8
38) 9 × 7
39) 7 × 3
40) 6 × 7
41) 7 × 6
42) 3 × 7

43) 7 × 2
44) 12 × 7
45) 7 × 12
46) 12 × 7
47) 7 × 3
48) 8 × 7
49) 7 × 6

50) 9 × 7
51) 7 × 10
52) 2 × 7
53) 7 × 10
54) 7 × 7
55) 7 × 12
56) 3 × 7

57) 7 × 7
58) 8 × 7
59) 7 × 12
60) 11 × 7

Time :

Score /60

DAY 50
· Multiplying 7 ·

1) 7 × 2
2) 4 × 7
3) 7 × 8
4) 6 × 7
5) 7 × 9
6) 1 × 7
7) 7 × 12

8) 9 × 7
9) 7 × 3
10) 6 × 7
11) 7 × 5
12) 11 × 7
13) 7 × 6
14) 4 × 7

15) 7 × 8
16) 2 × 7
17) 7 × 0
18) 9 × 7
19) 7 × 4
20) 12 × 7
21) 7 × 7

22) 9 × 7
23) 7 × 9
24) 10 × 7
25) 7 × 2
26) 9 × 7
27) 7 × 12
28) 3 × 7

29) 7 × 9
30) 11 × 7
31) 7 × 12
32) 7 × 7
33) 7 × 6
34) 4 × 7
35) 7 × 1

36) 1 × 7
37) 7 × 6
38) 8 × 7
39) 7 × 3
40) 5 × 7
41) 7 × 0
42) 1 × 7

43) 7 × 8
44) 3 × 7
45) 7 × 10
46) 7 × 7
47) 7 × 0
48) 11 × 7
49) 7 × 2

50) 4 × 7
51) 7 × 7
52) 5 × 7
53) 7 × 11
54) 12 × 7
55) 7 × 12
56) 11 × 7

57) 7 × 2
58) 7 × 7
59) 7 × 12
60) 0 × 7

Time :

Score /60

DAY 51
· Multiplying 7 ·

1) 7 × 12

2) 2 × 7

3) 7 × 7

4) 7 × 0

5) 7 × 6

6) 4 × 7

7) 7 × 6

8) 4 × 7

9) 7 × 9

10) 2 × 7

11) 7 × 4

12) 8 × 7

13) 7 × 5

14) 11 × 7

15) 7 × 11

16) 5 × 7

17) 7 × 12

18) 10 × 7

19) 7 × 8

20) 9 × 7

21) 7 × 6

22) 9 × 7

23) 7 × 8

24) 7 × 7

25) 7 × 6

26) 8 × 7

27) 7 × 10

28) 12 × 7

29) 7 × 8

30) 10 × 7

31) 7 × 5

32) 12 × 7

33) 7 × 10

34) 9 × 7

35) 7 × 10

36) 8 × 7

37) 7 × 11

38) 12 × 7

39) 7 × 11

40) 5 × 7

41) 7 × 9

42) 10 × 7

43) 7 × 4

44) 11 × 7

45) 7 × 6

46) 7 × 7

47) 7 × 9

48) 12 × 7

49) 7 × 7

50) 6 × 7

51) 7 × 8

52) 8 × 7

53) 7 × 8

54) 8 × 7

55) 7 × 6

56) 4 × 7

57) 7 × 11

58) 6 × 7

59) 7 × 9

60) 2 × 7

Time
:

Score
/60

QUESTION: HOW MANY DIFFERENT NAMES ARE THERE FOR THE NUMBER 0?

Answer: 6! These are zero, nought (or naught), nil, zilch, and zip.

The number 0 was originally called cipher. The word cipher comes from the Arabic word 'sifr', which translated to 'cifra' through Spanish and then cipher in modern English.

There is also another name used for the number 0 that is not quite as formal, and you may have already guessed it. It's 'oh'! Think about James Bond's agent number, 007. You probably read that as 'double oh seven', didn't you!

DAY 52
· Multiplying 8 ·

1) 8
  × 6

2) 7
  × 8

3) 8
  × 5

4) 7
  × 8

5) 8
  × 4

6) 3
  × 8

7) 8
  × 7

8) 5
  × 8

9) 8
  × 7

10) 4
  × 8

11) 8
  × 6

12) 2
  × 8

13) 8
  × 6

14) 9
  × 8

15) 8
  × 3

16) 9
  × 8

17) 8
  × 2

18) 3
  × 8

19) 8
  × 2

20) 9
  × 8

21) 8
  × 7

22) 9
  × 8

23) 8
  × 9

24) 2
  × 8

25) 8
  × 4

26) 5
  × 8

27) 8
  × 5

28) 9
  × 8

29) 8
  × 3

30) 7
  × 8

31) 8
  × 6

32) 8
  × 8

33) 8
  × 5

34) 6
  × 8

35) 8
  × 7

36) 9
  × 8

37) 8
  × 9

38) 7
  × 8

39) 8
  × 5

40) 4
  × 8

41) 8
  × 3

42) 4
  × 8

43) 8
  × 4

44) 4
  × 8

45) 8
  × 8

46) 6
  × 8

47) 8
  × 9

48) 3
  × 8

49) 8
  × 4

50) 9
  × 8

51) 8
  × 4

52) 4
  × 8

53) 8
  × 8

54) 8
  × 8

55) 8
  × 6

56) 4
  × 8

57) 8
  × 9

58) 4
  × 8

59) 8
  × 2

60) 4
  × 8

Time :

Score

/60

DAY 53
· Multiplying 8 ·

1) 8 × 7

2) 7 × 8

3) 8 × 1

4) 7 × 8

5) 8 × 8

6) 9 × 8

7) 8 × 7

8) 4 × 8

9) 8 × 3

10) 5 × 8

11) 8 × 1

12) 1 × 8

13) 8 × 8

14) 1 × 8

15) 8 × 4

16) 2 × 8

17) 8 × 3

18) 7 × 8

19) 8 × 3

20) 4 × 8

21) 8 × 0

22) 2 × 8

23) 8 × 1

24) 0 × 8

25) 8 × 2

26) 2 × 8

27) 8 × 2

28) 2 × 8

29) 8 × 2

30) 8 × 8

31) 8 × 7

32) 1 × 8

33) 8 × 0

34) 8 × 8

35) 8 × 0

36) 2 × 8

37) 8 × 1

38) 6 × 8

39) 8 × 5

40) 1 × 8

41) 8 × 3

42) 7 × 8

43) 8 × 7

44) 5 × 8

45) 8 × 5

46) 7 × 8

47) 8 × 7

48) 5 × 8

49) 8 × 8

50) 9 × 8

51) 8 × 3

52) 3 × 8

53) 8 × 6

54) 0 × 8

55) 8 × 1

56) 3 × 8

57) 8 × 7

58) 6 × 8

59) 8 × 7

60) 7 × 8

Time :

Score /60

DAY 54
· Multiplying 8 ·

1) 8 × 8

2) 7 × 8

3) 8 × 2

4) 8 × 8

5) 8 × 8

6) 2 × 8

7) 8 × 7

8) 9 × 8

9) 8 × 5

10) 9 × 8

11) 8 × 7

12) 8 × 8

13) 8 × 3

14) 9 × 8

15) 8 × 9

16) 8 × 8

17) 8 × 7

18) 6 × 8

19) 8 × 7

20) 4 × 8

21) 8 × 7

22) 9 × 8

23) 8 × 6

24) 4 × 8

25) 8 × 3

26) 8 × 8

27) 8 × 6

28) 8 × 8

29) 8 × 2

30) 5 × 8

31) 8 × 7

32) 2 × 8

33) 8 × 5

34) 9 × 8

35) 8 × 3

36) 9 × 8

37) 8 × 5

38) 4 × 8

39) 8 × 6

40) 3 × 8

41) 8 × 3

42) 2 × 8

43) 8 × 9

44) 2 × 8

45) 8 × 5

46) 8 × 8

47) 8 × 3

48) 2 × 8

49) 8 × 6

50) 7 × 8

51) 8 × 3

52) 4 × 8

53) 8 × 3

54) 6 × 8

55) 8 × 6

56) 9 × 8

57) 8 × 6

58) 7 × 8

59) 8 × 4

60) 5 × 8

Time :

Score

/60

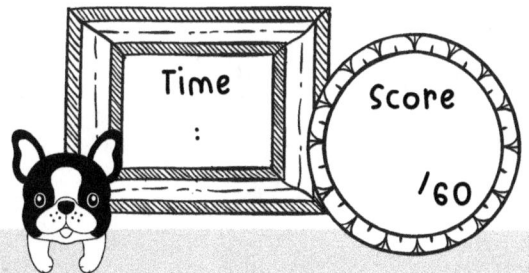

DAY 55
· Multiplying 8 ·

1) 8 × 6
2) 8 × 8
3) 8 × 9
4) 5 × 8
5) 8 × 6
6) 3 × 8
7) 8 × 5

8) 9 × 8
9) 8 × 4
10) 6 × 8
11) 8 × 2
12) 4 × 8
13) 8 × 4
14) 7 × 8

15) 8 × 4
16) 7 × 8
17) 8 × 9
18) 8 × 8
19) 8 × 6
20) 7 × 8
21) 8 × 4

22) 6 × 8
23) 8 × 7
24) 8 × 8
25) 8 × 7
26) 6 × 8
27) 8 × 2
28) 4 × 8

29) 8 × 3
30) 3 × 8
31) 8 × 7
32) 6 × 8
33) 8 × 8
34) 7 × 8
35) 8 × 9

36) 8 × 8
37) 8 × 5
38) 7 × 8
39) 8 × 4
40) 5 × 8
41) 8 × 7
42) 7 × 8

43) 8 × 2
44) 9 × 8
45) 8 × 3
46) 4 × 8
47) 8 × 9
48) 4 × 8
49) 8 × 4

50) 9 × 8
51) 8 × 3
52) 6 × 8
53) 8 × 7
54) 9 × 8
55) 8 × 9
56) 4 × 8

57) 8 × 6
58) 3 × 8
59) 8 × 6
60) 7 × 8

Time
:

Score
/60

DAY 56
· Multiplying 8 ·

1) 8 × 8
2) 11 × 8
3) 8 × 2
4) 1 × 8
5) 8 × 7
6) 4 × 8
7) 8 × 1

8) 6 × 8
9) 8 × 1
10) 9 × 8
11) 8 × 10
12) 5 × 8
13) 8 × 5
14) 11 × 8

15) 8 × 8
16) 1 × 8
17) 8 × 4
18) 3 × 8
19) 8 × 10
20) 4 × 8
21) 8 × 6

22) 4 × 8
23) 8 × 9
24) 3 × 8
25) 8 × 6
26) 12 × 8
27) 8 × 4
28) 11 × 8

29) 8 × 4
30) 10 × 8
31) 8 × 2
32) 10 × 8
33) 8 × 5
34) 7 × 8
35) 8 × 10

36) 9 × 8
37) 8 × 12
38) 7 × 8
39) 8 × 3
40) 0 × 8
41) 8 × 10
42) 8 × 8

43) 8 × 6
44) 10 × 8
45) 8 × 3
46) 2 × 8
47) 8 × 10
48) 11 × 8
49) 8 × 12

50) 10 × 8
51) 8 × 12
52) 9 × 8
53) 8 × 10
54) 10 × 8
55) 8 × 9
56) 1 × 8

57) 8 × 10
58) 9 × 8
59) 8 × 0
60) 0 × 8

Time :

Score /60

DAY 57
· Multiplying 8 ·

1) 8 × 5

2) 5 × 8

3) 8 × 8

4) 10 × 8

5) 8 × 12

6) 8 × 8

7) 8 × 10

8) 3 × 8

9) 8 × 7

10) 3 × 8

11) 8 × 2

12) 7 × 8

13) 8 × 3

14) 12 × 8

15) 8 × 3

16) 4 × 8

17) 8 × 10

18) 6 × 8

19) 8 × 2

20) 5 × 8

21) 8 × 9

22) 3 × 8

23) 8 × 6

24) 9 × 8

25) 8 × 5

26) 11 × 8

27) 8 × 6

28) 3 × 8

29) 8 × 11

30) 3 × 8

31) 8 × 12

32) 12 × 8

33) 8 × 8

34) 4 × 8

35) 8 × 8

36) 4 × 8

37) 8 × 11

38) 5 × 8

39) 8 × 4

40) 3 × 8

41) 8 × 4

42) 12 × 8

43) 8 × 10

44) 4 × 8

45) 8 × 8

46) 9 × 8

47) 8 × 7

48) 8 × 8

49) 8 × 8

50) 5 × 8

51) 8 × 8

52) 7 × 8

53) 8 × 12

54) 5 × 8

55) 8 × 3

56) 3 × 8

57) 8 × 4

58) 5 × 8

59) 8 × 11

60) 10 × 8

Time :

Score /60

DAY 58

· Multiplying 8 ·

1) 8
  × 6

2) 7
  × 8

3) 8
  × 4

4) 6
  × 8

5) 8
  × 5

6) 7
  × 8

7) 8
  × 10

8) 7
  × 8

9) 8
  × 4

10) 2
  × 8

11) 8
  × 9

12) 7
  × 8

13) 8
  × 4

14) 2
  × 8

15) 8
  × 6

16) 10
  × 8

17) 8
  × 7

18) 4
  × 8

19) 8
  × 12

20) 12
  × 8

21) 8
  × 12

22) 7
  × 8

23) 8
  × 9

24) 9
  × 8

25) 8
  × 11

26) 4
  × 8

27) 8
  × 9

28) 12
  × 8

29) 8
  × 7

30) 9
  × 8

31) 8
  × 6

32) 4
  × 8

33) 8
  × 3

34) 8
  × 8

35) 8
  × 8

36) 8
  × 8

37) 8
  × 9

38) 6
  × 8

39) 8
  × 11

40) 4
  × 8

41) 8
  × 8

42) 2
  × 8

43) 8
  × 4

44) 6
  × 8

45) 8
  × 3

46) 3
  × 8

47) 8
  × 7

48) 9
  × 8

49) 8
  × 4

50) 6
  × 8

51) 8
  × 6

52) 4
  × 8

53) 8
  × 3

54) 2
  × 8

55) 8
  × 12

56) 7
  × 8

57) 8
  × 3

58) 10
  × 8

59) 8
  × 9

60) 6
  × 8

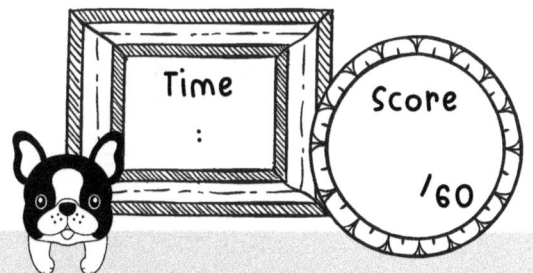

Time
:

Score

/60

DAY 59
· Multiplying 8 ·

1)   8
  × 11

2) 11
  × 8

3)   8
  × 9

4)   2
  × 8

5)   8
  × 8

6) 10
  × 8

7)   8
  × 12

8) 10
  × 8

9)   8
  × 11

10) 11
  × 8

11)   8
  × 2

12) 12
  × 8

13)   8
  × 12

14)   6
  × 8

15)   8
  × 10

16)   4
  × 8

17)   8
  × 4

18)   3
  × 8

19)   8
  × 11

20)   3
  × 8

21)   8
  × 4

22)   7
  × 8

23)   8
  × 10

24)   9
  × 8

25)   8
  × 9

26)   2
  × 8

27)   8
  × 10

28)   4
  × 8

29)   8
  × 2

30)   6
  × 8

31)   8
  × 9

32) 10
  × 8

33)   8
  × 8

34) 10
  × 8

35)   8
  × 10

36)   6
  × 8

37)   8
  × 9

38)   8
  × 8

39)   8
  × 11

40)   9
  × 8

41)   8
  × 9

42)   4
  × 8

43)   8
  × 12

44)   2
  × 8

45)   8
  × 12

46)   3
  × 8

47)   8
  × 4

48)   2
  × 8

49)   8
  × 7

50)   7
  × 8

51)   8
  × 11

52)   2
  × 8

53)   8
  × 12

54) 11
  × 8

55)   8
  × 5

56)   7
  × 8

57)   8
  × 8

58)   7
  × 8

59)   8
  × 7

60) 12
  × 8

Time :

Score /60

Back when I was looking at names for 0, I got my nose on the scent of some really interesting computer history!

Have you ever heard of Alan Turing? He was a British mathematician and computer scientist whose job during World War II was to crack German ciphers. These ciphers were not just the number 0. They were really complicated!

Ciphers were secret codes that turned normal text into something that could only be read by someone with the same cipher. How amazing is that?

Alan Turing's work contributed a lot to mathematical logic which played a very important role in the development of algorithms and the modern computer!

DAY 60
· Multiplying 9 ·

1) 9 × 7

2) 9 × 9

3) 9 × 8

4) 4 × 9

5) 9 × 3

6) 2 × 9

7) 9 × 7

8) 6 × 9

9) 9 × 7

10) 3 × 9

11) 9 × 2

12) 8 × 9

13) 9 × 7

14) 5 × 9

15) 9 × 9

16) 7 × 9

17) 9 × 8

18) 9 × 9

19) 9 × 6

20) 5 × 9

21) 9 × 8

22) 3 × 9

23) 9 × 6

24) 9 × 9

25) 9 × 5

26) 2 × 9

27) 9 × 3

28) 2 × 9

29) 9 × 6

30) 5 × 9

31) 9 × 5

32) 9 × 9

33) 9 × 7

34) 9 × 9

35) 9 × 4

36) 5 × 9

37) 9 × 2

38) 4 × 9

39) 9 × 5

40) 3 × 9

41) 9 × 2

42) 9 × 9

43) 9 × 6

44) 4 × 9

45) 9 × 3

46) 9 × 9

47) 9 × 7

48) 6 × 9

49) 9 × 2

50) 4 × 9

51) 9 × 2

52) 4 × 9

53) 9 × 8

54) 6 × 9

55) 9 × 6

56) 2 × 9

57) 9 × 4

58) 2 × 9

59) 9 × 4

60) 7 × 9

Time :

Score
/60

DAY 61

· Multiplying 9 ·

1)　　9　　　2)　　4　　　3)　　9　　　4)　　6　　　5)　　9　　　6)　　2　　　7)　　9
　　× 6　　　　× 9　　　　× 1　　　　× 9　　　　× 2　　　　× 9　　　　× 2

8)　　7　　　9)　　9　　　10)　　0　　　11)　　9　　　12)　　8　　　13)　　9　　　14)　　0
　　× 9　　　　× 3　　　　× 9　　　　× 6　　　　× 9　　　　× 5　　　　× 9

15)　　9　　　16)　　7　　　17)　　9　　　18)　　3　　　19)　　9　　　20)　　5　　　21)　　9
　　× 9　　　　× 9　　　　× 2　　　　× 9　　　　× 7　　　　× 9　　　　× 4

22)　　9　　　23)　　9　　　24)　　9　　　25)　　9　　　26)　　1　　　27)　　9　　　28)　　0
　　× 9　　　　× 1　　　　× 9　　　　× 3　　　　× 9　　　　× 4　　　　× 9

29)　　9　　　30)　　6　　　31)　　9　　　32)　　3　　　33)　　9　　　34)　　3　　　35)　　9
　　× 4　　　　× 9　　　　× 8　　　　× 9　　　　× 4　　　　× 9　　　　× 2

36)　　7　　　37)　　9　　　38)　　6　　　39)　　9　　　40)　　6　　　41)　　9　　　42)　　3
　　× 9　　　　× 2　　　　× 9　　　　× 6　　　　× 9　　　　× 4　　　　× 9

43)　　9　　　44)　　4　　　45)　　9　　　46)　　3　　　47)　　9　　　48)　　3　　　49)　　9
　　× 1　　　　× 9　　　　× 2　　　　× 9　　　　× 2　　　　× 9　　　　× 2

50)　　1　　　51)　　9　　　52)　　7　　　53)　　9　　　54)　　5　　　55)　　9　　　56)　　3
　　× 9　　　　× 5　　　　× 9　　　　× 6　　　　× 9　　　　× 4　　　　× 9

57)　　9　　　58)　　2　　　59)　　9　　　60)　　9
　　× 3　　　　× 9　　　　× 9　　　　× 3

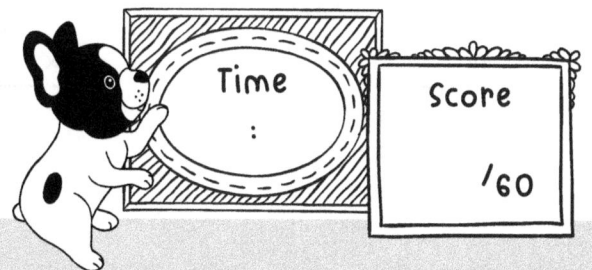

Time
:

Score

/60

DAY 62

· Multiplying 9 ·

1) 9
 × 5

2) 6
 × 9

3) 9
 × 4

4) 4
 × 9

5) 9
 × 7

6) 8
 × 9

7) 9
 × 3

8) 5
 × 9

9) 9
 × 7

10) 4
 × 9

11) 9
 × 2

12) 8
 × 9

13) 9
 × 4

14) 7
 × 9

15) 9
 × 8

16) 8
 × 9

17) 9
 × 9

18) 3
 × 9

19) 9
 × 3

20) 6
 × 9

21) 9
 × 7

22) 3
 × 9

23) 9
 × 7

24) 2
 × 9

25) 9
 × 5

26) 7
 × 9

27) 9
 × 8

28) 6
 × 9

29) 9
 × 9

30) 5
 × 9

31) 9
 × 9

32) 6
 × 9

33) 9
 × 3

34) 5
 × 9

35) 9
 × 8

36) 7
 × 9

37) 9
 × 7

38) 5
 × 9

39) 9
 × 2

40) 3
 × 9

41) 9
 × 7

42) 7
 × 9

43) 9
 × 2

44) 3
 × 9

45) 9
 × 7

46) 7
 × 9

47) 9
 × 2

48) 4
 × 9

49) 9
 × 6

50) 3
 × 9

51) 9
 × 3

52) 6
 × 9

53) 9
 × 7

54) 8
 × 9

55) 9
 × 3

56) 5
 × 9

57) 9
 × 3

58) 7
 × 9

59) 9
 × 5

60) 7
 × 9

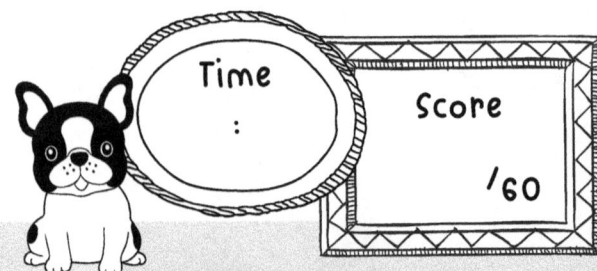

Time
:

Score

/60

DAY 63
· Multiplying 9 ·

1) $\begin{array}{r} 9 \\ \times\ 2 \\ \hline \end{array}$
2) $\begin{array}{r} 7 \\ \times\ 9 \\ \hline \end{array}$
3) $\begin{array}{r} 9 \\ \times\ 4 \\ \hline \end{array}$
4) $\begin{array}{r} 4 \\ \times\ 9 \\ \hline \end{array}$
5) $\begin{array}{r} 9 \\ \times\ 4 \\ \hline \end{array}$
6) $\begin{array}{r} 7 \\ \times\ 9 \\ \hline \end{array}$
7) $\begin{array}{r} 9 \\ \times\ 5 \\ \hline \end{array}$

8) $\begin{array}{r} 5 \\ \times\ 9 \\ \hline \end{array}$
9) $\begin{array}{r} 9 \\ \times\ 9 \\ \hline \end{array}$
10) $\begin{array}{r} 4 \\ \times\ 9 \\ \hline \end{array}$
11) $\begin{array}{r} 9 \\ \times\ 5 \\ \hline \end{array}$
12) $\begin{array}{r} 3 \\ \times\ 9 \\ \hline \end{array}$
13) $\begin{array}{r} 9 \\ \times\ 3 \\ \hline \end{array}$
14) $\begin{array}{r} 3 \\ \times\ 9 \\ \hline \end{array}$

15) $\begin{array}{r} 9 \\ \times\ 7 \\ \hline \end{array}$
16) $\begin{array}{r} 8 \\ \times\ 9 \\ \hline \end{array}$
17) $\begin{array}{r} 9 \\ \times\ 6 \\ \hline \end{array}$
18) $\begin{array}{r} 2 \\ \times\ 9 \\ \hline \end{array}$
19) $\begin{array}{r} 9 \\ \times\ 8 \\ \hline \end{array}$
20) $\begin{array}{r} 9 \\ \times\ 9 \\ \hline \end{array}$
21) $\begin{array}{r} 9 \\ \times\ 6 \\ \hline \end{array}$

22) $\begin{array}{r} 5 \\ \times\ 9 \\ \hline \end{array}$
23) $\begin{array}{r} 9 \\ \times\ 2 \\ \hline \end{array}$
24) $\begin{array}{r} 3 \\ \times\ 9 \\ \hline \end{array}$
25) $\begin{array}{r} 9 \\ \times\ 5 \\ \hline \end{array}$
26) $\begin{array}{r} 4 \\ \times\ 9 \\ \hline \end{array}$
27) $\begin{array}{r} 9 \\ \times\ 6 \\ \hline \end{array}$
28) $\begin{array}{r} 9 \\ \times\ 9 \\ \hline \end{array}$

29) $\begin{array}{r} 9 \\ \times\ 2 \\ \hline \end{array}$
30) $\begin{array}{r} 6 \\ \times\ 9 \\ \hline \end{array}$
31) $\begin{array}{r} 9 \\ \times\ 3 \\ \hline \end{array}$
32) $\begin{array}{r} 6 \\ \times\ 9 \\ \hline \end{array}$
33) $\begin{array}{r} 9 \\ \times\ 7 \\ \hline \end{array}$
34) $\begin{array}{r} 4 \\ \times\ 9 \\ \hline \end{array}$
35) $\begin{array}{r} 9 \\ \times\ 2 \\ \hline \end{array}$

36) $\begin{array}{r} 3 \\ \times\ 9 \\ \hline \end{array}$
37) $\begin{array}{r} 9 \\ \times\ 5 \\ \hline \end{array}$
38) $\begin{array}{r} 2 \\ \times\ 9 \\ \hline \end{array}$
39) $\begin{array}{r} 9 \\ \times\ 6 \\ \hline \end{array}$
40) $\begin{array}{r} 3 \\ \times\ 9 \\ \hline \end{array}$
41) $\begin{array}{r} 9 \\ \times\ 6 \\ \hline \end{array}$
42) $\begin{array}{r} 8 \\ \times\ 9 \\ \hline \end{array}$

43) $\begin{array}{r} 9 \\ \times\ 5 \\ \hline \end{array}$
44) $\begin{array}{r} 5 \\ \times\ 9 \\ \hline \end{array}$
45) $\begin{array}{r} 9 \\ \times\ 4 \\ \hline \end{array}$
46) $\begin{array}{r} 9 \\ \times\ 9 \\ \hline \end{array}$
47) $\begin{array}{r} 9 \\ \times\ 8 \\ \hline \end{array}$
48) $\begin{array}{r} 2 \\ \times\ 9 \\ \hline \end{array}$
49) $\begin{array}{r} 9 \\ \times\ 3 \\ \hline \end{array}$

50) $\begin{array}{r} 3 \\ \times\ 9 \\ \hline \end{array}$
51) $\begin{array}{r} 9 \\ \times\ 5 \\ \hline \end{array}$
52) $\begin{array}{r} 7 \\ \times\ 9 \\ \hline \end{array}$
53) $\begin{array}{r} 9 \\ \times\ 5 \\ \hline \end{array}$
54) $\begin{array}{r} 3 \\ \times\ 9 \\ \hline \end{array}$
55) $\begin{array}{r} 9 \\ \times\ 6 \\ \hline \end{array}$
56) $\begin{array}{r} 3 \\ \times\ 9 \\ \hline \end{array}$

57) $\begin{array}{r} 9 \\ \times\ 2 \\ \hline \end{array}$
58) $\begin{array}{r} 8 \\ \times\ 9 \\ \hline \end{array}$
59) $\begin{array}{r} 9 \\ \times\ 9 \\ \hline \end{array}$
60) $\begin{array}{r} 5 \\ \times\ 9 \\ \hline \end{array}$

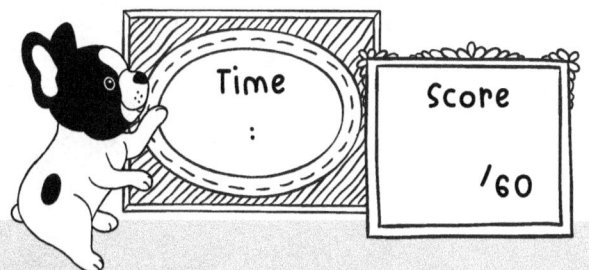

Time
:

Score
/60

DAY 64
· Multiplying 9 ·

1)   9
   × 4

2)   9
   × 9

3)   9
   × 10

4)   4
   × 9

5)   9
  × 12

6)   8
   × 9

7)   9
   × 8

8)   8
   × 9

9)   9
   × 8

10)   8
   × 9

11)   9
   × 9

12)   2
   × 9

13)   9
  × 11

14)   2
   × 9

15)   9
  × 10

16)   2
   × 9

17)   9
  × 12

18) 10
   × 9

19)   9
  × 10

20) 12
   × 9

21)   9
   × 5

22) 12
   × 9

23)   9
   × 4

24) 11
   × 9

25)   9
   × 5

26)   9
   × 9

27)   9
   × 6

28)   6
   × 9

29)   9
   × 5

30)   2
   × 9

31)   9
   × 2

32) 12
   × 9

33)   9
   × 5

34)   6
   × 9

35)   9
   × 9

36) 10
   × 9

37)   9
   × 8

38)   7
   × 9

39)   9
  × 12

40)   2
   × 9

41)   9
  × 10

42) 11
   × 9

43)   9
  × 10

44)   8
   × 9

45)   9
  × 10

46)   5
   × 9

47)   9
   × 2

48)   8
   × 9

49)   9
  × 10

50)   2
   × 9

51)   9
   × 6

52)   5
   × 9

53)   9
   × 4

54) 11
   × 9

55)   9
   × 8

56) 11
   × 9

57)   9
  × 10

58)   8
   × 9

59)   9
   × 8

60)   5
   × 9

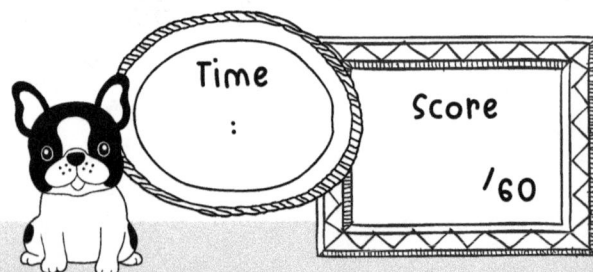

Time
:

Score
/60

DAY 65
· Multiplying 9 ·

1) $\begin{array}{r} 9 \\ \times\ 8 \\ \hline \end{array}$
2) $\begin{array}{r} 8 \\ \times\ 9 \\ \hline \end{array}$
3) $\begin{array}{r} 9 \\ \times\ 4 \\ \hline \end{array}$
4) $\begin{array}{r} 2 \\ \times\ 9 \\ \hline \end{array}$
5) $\begin{array}{r} 9 \\ \times\ 11 \\ \hline \end{array}$
6) $\begin{array}{r} 10 \\ \times\ 9 \\ \hline \end{array}$
7) $\begin{array}{r} 9 \\ \times\ 3 \\ \hline \end{array}$

8) $\begin{array}{r} 5 \\ \times\ 9 \\ \hline \end{array}$
9) $\begin{array}{r} 9 \\ \times\ 3 \\ \hline \end{array}$
10) $\begin{array}{r} 11 \\ \times\ 9 \\ \hline \end{array}$
11) $\begin{array}{r} 9 \\ \times\ 5 \\ \hline \end{array}$
12) $\begin{array}{r} 3 \\ \times\ 9 \\ \hline \end{array}$
13) $\begin{array}{r} 9 \\ \times\ 5 \\ \hline \end{array}$
14) $\begin{array}{r} 5 \\ \times\ 9 \\ \hline \end{array}$

15) $\begin{array}{r} 9 \\ \times\ 9 \\ \hline \end{array}$
16) $\begin{array}{r} 5 \\ \times\ 9 \\ \hline \end{array}$
17) $\begin{array}{r} 9 \\ \times\ 10 \\ \hline \end{array}$
18) $\begin{array}{r} 4 \\ \times\ 9 \\ \hline \end{array}$
19) $\begin{array}{r} 9 \\ \times\ 12 \\ \hline \end{array}$
20) $\begin{array}{r} 2 \\ \times\ 9 \\ \hline \end{array}$
21) $\begin{array}{r} 9 \\ \times\ 6 \\ \hline \end{array}$

22) $\begin{array}{r} 7 \\ \times\ 9 \\ \hline \end{array}$
23) $\begin{array}{r} 9 \\ \times\ 11 \\ \hline \end{array}$
24) $\begin{array}{r} 9 \\ \times\ 9 \\ \hline \end{array}$
25) $\begin{array}{r} 9 \\ \times\ 8 \\ \hline \end{array}$
26) $\begin{array}{r} 7 \\ \times\ 9 \\ \hline \end{array}$
27) $\begin{array}{r} 9 \\ \times\ 4 \\ \hline \end{array}$
28) $\begin{array}{r} 8 \\ \times\ 9 \\ \hline \end{array}$

29) $\begin{array}{r} 9 \\ \times\ 3 \\ \hline \end{array}$
30) $\begin{array}{r} 7 \\ \times\ 9 \\ \hline \end{array}$
31) $\begin{array}{r} 9 \\ \times\ 11 \\ \hline \end{array}$
32) $\begin{array}{r} 12 \\ \times\ 9 \\ \hline \end{array}$
33) $\begin{array}{r} 9 \\ \times\ 3 \\ \hline \end{array}$
34) $\begin{array}{r} 3 \\ \times\ 9 \\ \hline \end{array}$
35) $\begin{array}{r} 9 \\ \times\ 5 \\ \hline \end{array}$

36) $\begin{array}{r} 12 \\ \times\ 9 \\ \hline \end{array}$
37) $\begin{array}{r} 9 \\ \times\ 11 \\ \hline \end{array}$
38) $\begin{array}{r} 12 \\ \times\ 9 \\ \hline \end{array}$
39) $\begin{array}{r} 9 \\ \times\ 11 \\ \hline \end{array}$
40) $\begin{array}{r} 12 \\ \times\ 9 \\ \hline \end{array}$
41) $\begin{array}{r} 9 \\ \times\ 4 \\ \hline \end{array}$
42) $\begin{array}{r} 12 \\ \times\ 9 \\ \hline \end{array}$

43) $\begin{array}{r} 9 \\ \times\ 7 \\ \hline \end{array}$
44) $\begin{array}{r} 4 \\ \times\ 9 \\ \hline \end{array}$
45) $\begin{array}{r} 9 \\ \times\ 2 \\ \hline \end{array}$
46) $\begin{array}{r} 3 \\ \times\ 9 \\ \hline \end{array}$
47) $\begin{array}{r} 9 \\ \times\ 10 \\ \hline \end{array}$
48) $\begin{array}{r} 5 \\ \times\ 9 \\ \hline \end{array}$
49) $\begin{array}{r} 9 \\ \times\ 11 \\ \hline \end{array}$

50) $\begin{array}{r} 4 \\ \times\ 9 \\ \hline \end{array}$
51) $\begin{array}{r} 9 \\ \times\ 8 \\ \hline \end{array}$
52) $\begin{array}{r} 5 \\ \times\ 9 \\ \hline \end{array}$
53) $\begin{array}{r} 9 \\ \times\ 12 \\ \hline \end{array}$
54) $\begin{array}{r} 6 \\ \times\ 9 \\ \hline \end{array}$
55) $\begin{array}{r} 9 \\ \times\ 11 \\ \hline \end{array}$
56) $\begin{array}{r} 11 \\ \times\ 9 \\ \hline \end{array}$

57) $\begin{array}{r} 9 \\ \times\ 12 \\ \hline \end{array}$
58) $\begin{array}{r} 11 \\ \times\ 9 \\ \hline \end{array}$
59) $\begin{array}{r} 9 \\ \times\ 4 \\ \hline \end{array}$
60) $\begin{array}{r} 8 \\ \times\ 9 \\ \hline \end{array}$

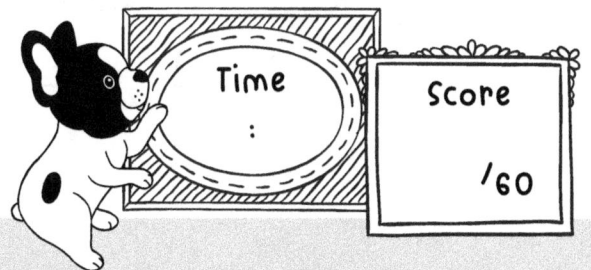

Time
:

Score

/60

DAY 66
· Multiplying 9 ·

1)　　　9　　2)　　　8　　3)　　　9　　4)　　　8　　5)　　　9　　6)　　　2　　7)　　　9
　　× 　2　　　× 　9　　　× 　4　　　× 　9　　　× 　7　　　× 　9　　　× 10

8)　　 10　　9)　　　9　　10)　　12　　11)　　　9　　12)　　　4　　13)　　　9　　14)　　　3
　　× 　9　　　× 12　　　× 　9　　　× 　9　　　× 　9　　　× 　0　　　× 　9

15)　　　9　　16)　　　4　　17)　　　9　　18)　　10　　19)　　　9　　20)　　　3　　21)　　　9
　　× 　7　　　× 　9　　　× 　6　　　× 　9　　　× 　3　　　× 　9　　　× 10

22)　　12　　23)　　　9　　24)　　　3　　25)　　　9　　26)　　　6　　27)　　　9　　28)　　　3
　　× 　9　　　× 12　　　× 　9　　　× 　4　　　× 　9　　　× 　4　　　× 　9

29)　　　9　　30)　　　4　　31)　　　9　　32)　　　0　　33)　　　9　　34)　　　8　　35)　　　9
　　× 　7　　　× 　9　　　× 　0　　　× 　9　　　× 11　　　× 　9　　　× 11

36)　　11　　37)　　　9　　38)　　　3　　39)　　　9　　40)　　　4　　41)　　　9　　42)　　　4
　　× 　9　　　× 12　　　× 　9　　　× 　3　　　× 　9　　　× 　8　　　× 　9

43)　　　9　　44)　　　4　　45)　　　9　　46)　　　9　　47)　　　9　　48)　　　9　　49)　　　9
　　× 　2　　　× 　9　　　× 　6　　　× 　9　　　× 　6　　　× 　9　　　× 　2

50)　　　4　　51)　　　9　　52)　　　0　　53)　　　9　　54)　　　1　　55)　　　9　　56)　　11
　　× 　9　　　× 12　　　× 　9　　　× 　5　　　× 　9　　　× 　7　　　× 　9

57)　　　9　　58)　　　6　　59)　　　9　　60)　　　0
　　× 　7　　　× 　9　　　× 　6　　　× 　9

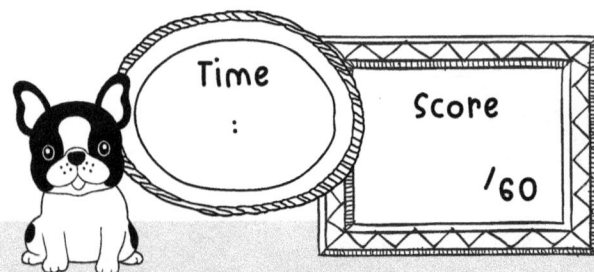

Time
:

Score
/60

DAY 67
· Multiplying 9 ·

1)   9
   × 7

2)   8
   × 9

3)   9
   × 9

4)   3
   × 9

5)   9
   × 6

6)   2
   × 9

7)   9
   × 3

8)   9
   × 9

9)   9
   × 6

10)   5
    × 9

11)   9
    × 5

12)   6
    × 9

13)   9
    × 9

14)   5
    × 9

15)   9
    × 6

16)   5
    × 9

17)   9
    × 9

18)   4
    × 9

19)   9
    × 12

20)   3
    × 9

21)   9
    × 9

22)   3
    × 9

23)   9
    × 5

24)   3
    × 9

25)   9
    × 6

26)   5
    × 9

27)   9
    × 11

28)   7
    × 9

29)   9
    × 9

30)   9
    × 9

31)   9
    × 4

32)   6
    × 9

33)   9
    × 3

34)   4
    × 9

35)   9
    × 2

36)   2
    × 9

37)   9
    × 4

38)   6
    × 9

39)   9
    × 5

40)   9
    × 9

41)   9
    × 3

42)   11
    × 9

43)   9
    × 2

44)   5
    × 9

45)   9
    × 11

46)   6
    × 9

47)   9
    × 9

48)   7
    × 9

49)   9
    × 12

50)   5
    × 9

51)   9
    × 5

52)   5
    × 9

53)   9
    × 2

54)   7
    × 9

55)   9
    × 12

56)   8
    × 9

57)   9
    × 7

58)   6
    × 9

59)   9
    × 9

60)   5
    × 9

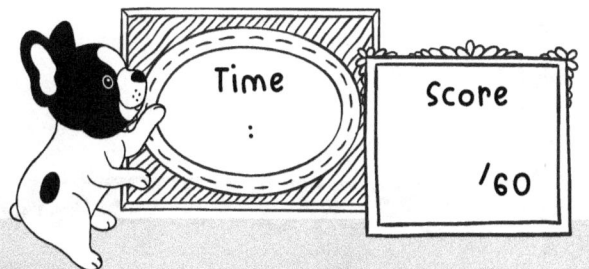

Time :

Score

/60

THE NUMBER NINE IS CONSIDERED A MAGIC NUMBER!

Who knew that magic could be involved in math?

This is because when we add up the digital sum (adding the single numbers together in a larger number until you have one number left) of any multiple of 9, you will get 9!

Let me show you:

$9 \times 9 = 81, 8 + 1 = 9$

$9 \times 99 = 891, 8 + 9 + 1 = 18, 1 + 8 = 9$

$27 \times 9 = 243, 2 + 4 + 3 = 9$

$99 \times 999 = 98,901, 9 + 8 + 9 + 0 + 1 = 27, 2 + 7 = 9$

Isn't that amazing?

DAY 68

· Multiplying 10 ·

1) $\begin{array}{r} 10 \\ \times\ \ 7 \\ \hline \end{array}$ 2) $\begin{array}{r} 5 \\ \times\ 10 \\ \hline \end{array}$ 3) $\begin{array}{r} 10 \\ \times\ \ 8 \\ \hline \end{array}$ 4) $\begin{array}{r} 7 \\ \times\ 10 \\ \hline \end{array}$ 5) $\begin{array}{r} 10 \\ \times\ \ 5 \\ \hline \end{array}$ 6) $\begin{array}{r} 8 \\ \times\ 10 \\ \hline \end{array}$ 7) $\begin{array}{r} 10 \\ \times\ \ 8 \\ \hline \end{array}$

8) $\begin{array}{r} 9 \\ \times\ 10 \\ \hline \end{array}$ 9) $\begin{array}{r} 10 \\ \times\ \ 8 \\ \hline \end{array}$ 10) $\begin{array}{r} 6 \\ \times\ 10 \\ \hline \end{array}$ 11) $\begin{array}{r} 10 \\ \times\ \ 3 \\ \hline \end{array}$ 12) $\begin{array}{r} 3 \\ \times\ 10 \\ \hline \end{array}$ 13) $\begin{array}{r} 10 \\ \times\ \ 6 \\ \hline \end{array}$ 14) $\begin{array}{r} 4 \\ \times\ 10 \\ \hline \end{array}$

15) $\begin{array}{r} 10 \\ \times\ \ 7 \\ \hline \end{array}$ 16) $\begin{array}{r} 9 \\ \times\ 10 \\ \hline \end{array}$ 17) $\begin{array}{r} 10 \\ \times\ \ 3 \\ \hline \end{array}$ 18) $\begin{array}{r} 9 \\ \times\ 10 \\ \hline \end{array}$ 19) $\begin{array}{r} 10 \\ \times\ \ 8 \\ \hline \end{array}$ 20) $\begin{array}{r} 9 \\ \times\ 10 \\ \hline \end{array}$ 21) $\begin{array}{r} 10 \\ \times\ \ 6 \\ \hline \end{array}$

22) $\begin{array}{r} 3 \\ \times\ 10 \\ \hline \end{array}$ 23) $\begin{array}{r} 10 \\ \times\ \ 5 \\ \hline \end{array}$ 24) $\begin{array}{r} 6 \\ \times\ 10 \\ \hline \end{array}$ 25) $\begin{array}{r} 10 \\ \times\ \ 6 \\ \hline \end{array}$ 26) $\begin{array}{r} 6 \\ \times\ 10 \\ \hline \end{array}$ 27) $\begin{array}{r} 10 \\ \times\ \ 6 \\ \hline \end{array}$ 28) $\begin{array}{r} 2 \\ \times\ 10 \\ \hline \end{array}$

29) $\begin{array}{r} 10 \\ \times\ \ 2 \\ \hline \end{array}$ 30) $\begin{array}{r} 8 \\ \times\ 10 \\ \hline \end{array}$ 31) $\begin{array}{r} 10 \\ \times\ \ 7 \\ \hline \end{array}$ 32) $\begin{array}{r} 3 \\ \times\ 10 \\ \hline \end{array}$ 33) $\begin{array}{r} 10 \\ \times\ \ 3 \\ \hline \end{array}$ 34) $\begin{array}{r} 7 \\ \times\ 10 \\ \hline \end{array}$ 35) $\begin{array}{r} 10 \\ \times\ \ 4 \\ \hline \end{array}$

36) $\begin{array}{r} 8 \\ \times\ 10 \\ \hline \end{array}$ 37) $\begin{array}{r} 10 \\ \times\ \ 4 \\ \hline \end{array}$ 38) $\begin{array}{r} 8 \\ \times\ 10 \\ \hline \end{array}$ 39) $\begin{array}{r} 10 \\ \times\ \ 6 \\ \hline \end{array}$ 40) $\begin{array}{r} 6 \\ \times\ 10 \\ \hline \end{array}$ 41) $\begin{array}{r} 10 \\ \times\ \ 4 \\ \hline \end{array}$ 42) $\begin{array}{r} 4 \\ \times\ 10 \\ \hline \end{array}$

43) $\begin{array}{r} 10 \\ \times\ \ 7 \\ \hline \end{array}$ 44) $\begin{array}{r} 3 \\ \times\ 10 \\ \hline \end{array}$ 45) $\begin{array}{r} 10 \\ \times\ \ 3 \\ \hline \end{array}$ 46) $\begin{array}{r} 9 \\ \times\ 10 \\ \hline \end{array}$ 47) $\begin{array}{r} 10 \\ \times\ \ 5 \\ \hline \end{array}$ 48) $\begin{array}{r} 6 \\ \times\ 10 \\ \hline \end{array}$ 49) $\begin{array}{r} 10 \\ \times\ \ 2 \\ \hline \end{array}$

50) $\begin{array}{r} 9 \\ \times\ 10 \\ \hline \end{array}$ 51) $\begin{array}{r} 10 \\ \times\ \ 2 \\ \hline \end{array}$ 52) $\begin{array}{r} 3 \\ \times\ 10 \\ \hline \end{array}$ 53) $\begin{array}{r} 10 \\ \times\ \ 3 \\ \hline \end{array}$ 54) $\begin{array}{r} 8 \\ \times\ 10 \\ \hline \end{array}$ 55) $\begin{array}{r} 10 \\ \times\ \ 5 \\ \hline \end{array}$ 56) $\begin{array}{r} 9 \\ \times\ 10 \\ \hline \end{array}$

57) $\begin{array}{r} 10 \\ \times\ \ 9 \\ \hline \end{array}$ 58) $\begin{array}{r} 3 \\ \times\ 10 \\ \hline \end{array}$ 59) $\begin{array}{r} 10 \\ \times\ \ 3 \\ \hline \end{array}$ 60) $\begin{array}{r} 6 \\ \times\ 10 \\ \hline \end{array}$

Time
:

Score

/60

DAY 69

· Multiplying 10 ·

1) $\begin{array}{r} 10 \\ \times\ 4 \\ \hline \end{array}$
2) $\begin{array}{r} 9 \\ \times\ 10 \\ \hline \end{array}$
3) $\begin{array}{r} 10 \\ \times\ 5 \\ \hline \end{array}$
4) $\begin{array}{r} 3 \\ \times\ 10 \\ \hline \end{array}$
5) $\begin{array}{r} 10 \\ \times\ 3 \\ \hline \end{array}$
6) $\begin{array}{r} 5 \\ \times\ 10 \\ \hline \end{array}$
7) $\begin{array}{r} 10 \\ \times\ 3 \\ \hline \end{array}$

8) $\begin{array}{r} 3 \\ \times\ 10 \\ \hline \end{array}$
9) $\begin{array}{r} 10 \\ \times\ 3 \\ \hline \end{array}$
10) $\begin{array}{r} 4 \\ \times\ 10 \\ \hline \end{array}$
11) $\begin{array}{r} 10 \\ \times\ 5 \\ \hline \end{array}$
12) $\begin{array}{r} 8 \\ \times\ 10 \\ \hline \end{array}$
13) $\begin{array}{r} 10 \\ \times\ 6 \\ \hline \end{array}$
14) $\begin{array}{r} 9 \\ \times\ 10 \\ \hline \end{array}$

15) $\begin{array}{r} 10 \\ \times\ 2 \\ \hline \end{array}$
16) $\begin{array}{r} 2 \\ \times\ 10 \\ \hline \end{array}$
17) $\begin{array}{r} 10 \\ \times\ 4 \\ \hline \end{array}$
18) $\begin{array}{r} 2 \\ \times\ 10 \\ \hline \end{array}$
19) $\begin{array}{r} 10 \\ \times\ 8 \\ \hline \end{array}$
20) $\begin{array}{r} 8 \\ \times\ 10 \\ \hline \end{array}$
21) $\begin{array}{r} 10 \\ \times\ 8 \\ \hline \end{array}$

22) $\begin{array}{r} 6 \\ \times\ 10 \\ \hline \end{array}$
23) $\begin{array}{r} 10 \\ \times\ 6 \\ \hline \end{array}$
24) $\begin{array}{r} 6 \\ \times\ 10 \\ \hline \end{array}$
25) $\begin{array}{r} 10 \\ \times\ 6 \\ \hline \end{array}$
26) $\begin{array}{r} 6 \\ \times\ 10 \\ \hline \end{array}$
27) $\begin{array}{r} 10 \\ \times\ 4 \\ \hline \end{array}$
28) $\begin{array}{r} 7 \\ \times\ 10 \\ \hline \end{array}$

29) $\begin{array}{r} 10 \\ \times\ 6 \\ \hline \end{array}$
30) $\begin{array}{r} 3 \\ \times\ 10 \\ \hline \end{array}$
31) $\begin{array}{r} 10 \\ \times\ 5 \\ \hline \end{array}$
32) $\begin{array}{r} 7 \\ \times\ 10 \\ \hline \end{array}$
33) $\begin{array}{r} 10 \\ \times\ 5 \\ \hline \end{array}$
34) $\begin{array}{r} 7 \\ \times\ 10 \\ \hline \end{array}$
35) $\begin{array}{r} 10 \\ \times\ 4 \\ \hline \end{array}$

36) $\begin{array}{r} 3 \\ \times\ 10 \\ \hline \end{array}$
37) $\begin{array}{r} 10 \\ \times\ 4 \\ \hline \end{array}$
38) $\begin{array}{r} 8 \\ \times\ 10 \\ \hline \end{array}$
39) $\begin{array}{r} 10 \\ \times\ 3 \\ \hline \end{array}$
40) $\begin{array}{r} 5 \\ \times\ 10 \\ \hline \end{array}$
41) $\begin{array}{r} 10 \\ \times\ 9 \\ \hline \end{array}$
42) $\begin{array}{r} 4 \\ \times\ 10 \\ \hline \end{array}$

43) $\begin{array}{r} 10 \\ \times\ 4 \\ \hline \end{array}$
44) $\begin{array}{r} 7 \\ \times\ 10 \\ \hline \end{array}$
45) $\begin{array}{r} 10 \\ \times\ 6 \\ \hline \end{array}$
46) $\begin{array}{r} 6 \\ \times\ 10 \\ \hline \end{array}$
47) $\begin{array}{r} 10 \\ \times\ 3 \\ \hline \end{array}$
48) $\begin{array}{r} 5 \\ \times\ 10 \\ \hline \end{array}$
49) $\begin{array}{r} 10 \\ \times\ 3 \\ \hline \end{array}$

50) $\begin{array}{r} 3 \\ \times\ 10 \\ \hline \end{array}$
51) $\begin{array}{r} 10 \\ \times\ 3 \\ \hline \end{array}$
52) $\begin{array}{r} 4 \\ \times\ 10 \\ \hline \end{array}$
53) $\begin{array}{r} 10 \\ \times\ 7 \\ \hline \end{array}$
54) $\begin{array}{r} 7 \\ \times\ 10 \\ \hline \end{array}$
55) $\begin{array}{r} 10 \\ \times\ 5 \\ \hline \end{array}$
56) $\begin{array}{r} 8 \\ \times\ 10 \\ \hline \end{array}$

57) $\begin{array}{r} 10 \\ \times\ 9 \\ \hline \end{array}$
58) $\begin{array}{r} 5 \\ \times\ 10 \\ \hline \end{array}$
59) $\begin{array}{r} 10 \\ \times\ 3 \\ \hline \end{array}$
60) $\begin{array}{r} 6 \\ \times\ 10 \\ \hline \end{array}$

Time :

Score /60

DAY 70
· Multiplying 10 ·

1) 10 × 6

2) 9 × 10

3) 10 × 3

4) 6 × 10

5) 10 × 6

6) 5 × 10

7) 10 × 1

8) 10 × 10

9) 10 × 7

10) 7 × 10

11) 10 × 8

12) 7 × 10

13) 10 × 12

14) 12 × 10

15) 10 × 6

16) 10 × 10

17) 10 × 8

18) 8 × 10

19) 10 × 1

20) 12 × 10

21) 10 × 12

22) 3 × 10

23) 10 × 9

24) 9 × 10

25) 10 × 7

26) 10 × 10

27) 10 × 2

28) 2 × 10

29) 10 × 7

30) 3 × 10

31) 10 × 2

32) 5 × 10

33) 10 × 4

34) 11 × 10

35) 10 × 1

36) 5 × 10

37) 10 × 12

38) 8 × 10

39) 10 × 2

40) 4 × 10

41) 10 × 8

42) 1 × 10

43) 10 × 10

44) 9 × 10

45) 10 × 8

46) 12 × 10

47) 10 × 1

48) 4 × 10

49) 10 × 4

50) 6 × 10

51) 10 × 11

52) 8 × 10

53) 10 × 8

54) 10 × 10

55) 10 × 10

56) 6 × 10

57) 10 × 12

58) 6 × 10

59) 10 × 5

60) 3 × 10

Time :

Score /60

DAY 71
· Multiplying 10 ·

1)   10   2)   5   3)   10   4)   4   5)   10   6)   8   7)   10
×   4   × 10   ×   9   × 10   ×   2   × 10   ×   2

8)   7   9)   10   10)   12   11)   10   12)   2   13)   10   14)   10
× 10   × 10   × 10   ×   5   × 10   × 12   × 10

15)   10   16)   12   17)   10   18)   4   19)   10   20)   11   21)   10
×   8   × 10   × 12   × 10   ×   7   × 10   ×   6

22)   5   23)   10   24)   6   25)   10   26)   2   27)   10   28)   12
× 10   ×   4   × 10   ×   5   × 10   ×   3   × 10

29)   10   30)   2   31)   10   32)   8   33)   10   34)   2   35)   10
× 11   × 10   ×   9   × 10   ×   9   × 10   ×   8

36)   5   37)   10   38)   3   39)   10   40)   10   41)   10   42)   3
× 10   ×   5   × 10   × 11   × 10   ×   3   × 10

43)   10   44)   11   45)   10   46)   3   47)   10   48)   2   49)   10
×   6   × 10   × 12   × 10   × 12   × 10   ×   9

50)   12   51)   10   52)   11   53)   10   54)   4   55)   10   56)   10
× 10   × 11   × 10   ×   7   × 10   ×   8   × 10

57)   10   58)   8   59)   10   60)   7
×   3   × 10   × 12   × 10

Time
:

Score
/60

DAY 72
· Multiplying 11 ·

1) 11
  × 5

2) 2
  × 11

3) 11
  × 3

4) 3
  × 11

5) 11
  × 6

6) 3
  × 11

7) 11
  × 2

8) 7
  × 11

9) 11
  × 2

10) 9
  × 11

11) 11
  × 2

12) 2
  × 11

13) 11
  × 5

14) 9
  × 11

15) 11
  × 4

16) 9
  × 11

17) 11
  × 5

18) 2
  × 11

19) 11
  × 6

20) 2
  × 11

21) 11
  × 3

22) 9
  × 11

23) 11
  × 2

24) 5
  × 11

25) 11
  × 7

26) 4
  × 11

27) 11
  × 4

28) 3
  × 11

29) 11
  × 8

30) 3
  × 11

31) 11
  × 9

32) 8
  × 11

33) 11
  × 7

34) 3
  × 11

35) 11
  × 3

36) 6
  × 11

37) 11
  × 5

38) 6
  × 11

39) 11
  × 3

40) 5
  × 11

41) 11
  × 7

42) 3
  × 11

43) 11
  × 6

44) 5
  × 11

45) 11
  × 5

46) 3
  × 11

47) 11
  × 5

48) 9
  × 11

49) 11
  × 3

50) 2
  × 11

51) 11
  × 8

52) 6
  × 11

53) 11
  × 8

54) 4
  × 11

55) 11
  × 6

56) 2
  × 11

57) 11
  × 4

58) 8
  × 11

59) 11
  × 8

60) 2
  × 11

Time
:

Score
/60

DAY 73
· Multiplying 11 ·

1)   11
   × 4

2)   8
   × 11

3)   11
   × 9

4)   4
   × 11

5)   11
   × 9

6)   4
   × 11

7)   11
   × 6

8)   9
   × 11

9)   11
   × 8

10)   8
   × 11

11)   11
   × 5

12)   6
   × 11

13)   11
   × 8

14)   5
   × 11

15)   11
   × 8

16)   7
   × 11

17)   11
   × 7

18)   6
   × 11

19)   11
   × 7

20)   7
   × 11

21)   11
   × 6

22)   7
   × 11

23)   11
   × 3

24)   3
   × 11

25)   11
   × 8

26)   5
   × 11

27)   11
   × 4

28)   5
   × 11

29)   11
   × 6

30)   6
   × 11

31)   11
   × 4

32)   4
   × 11

33)   11
   × 4

34)   6
   × 11

35)   11
   × 9

36)   5
   × 11

37)   11
   × 5

38)   4
   × 11

39)   11
   × 3

40)   3
   × 11

41)   11
   × 5

42)   8
   × 11

43)   11
   × 2

44)   3
   × 11

45)   11
   × 3

46)   9
   × 11

47)   11
   × 8

48)   8
   × 11

49)   11
   × 9

50)   8
   × 11

51)   11
   × 2

52)   8
   × 11

53)   11
   × 8

54)   8
   × 11

55)   11
   × 6

56)   2
   × 11

57)   11
   × 2

58)   9
   × 11

59)   11
   × 6

60)   9
   × 11

Time :

Score /60

DAY 74
· Multiplying 11 ·

1)
$$\begin{array}{r} 11 \\ \times\ 6 \\ \hline \end{array}$$

2)
$$\begin{array}{r} 9 \\ \times\ 11 \\ \hline \end{array}$$

3)
$$\begin{array}{r} 11 \\ \times\ 8 \\ \hline \end{array}$$

4)
$$\begin{array}{r} 1 \\ \times\ 11 \\ \hline \end{array}$$

5)
$$\begin{array}{r} 11 \\ \times\ 12 \\ \hline \end{array}$$

6)
$$\begin{array}{r} 1 \\ \times\ 11 \\ \hline \end{array}$$

7)
$$\begin{array}{r} 11 \\ \times\ 4 \\ \hline \end{array}$$

8)
$$\begin{array}{r} 7 \\ \times\ 11 \\ \hline \end{array}$$

9)
$$\begin{array}{r} 11 \\ \times\ 9 \\ \hline \end{array}$$

10)
$$\begin{array}{r} 9 \\ \times\ 11 \\ \hline \end{array}$$

11)
$$\begin{array}{r} 11 \\ \times\ 10 \\ \hline \end{array}$$

12)
$$\begin{array}{r} 7 \\ \times\ 11 \\ \hline \end{array}$$

13)
$$\begin{array}{r} 11 \\ \times\ 9 \\ \hline \end{array}$$

14)
$$\begin{array}{r} 10 \\ \times\ 11 \\ \hline \end{array}$$

15)
$$\begin{array}{r} 11 \\ \times\ 3 \\ \hline \end{array}$$

16)
$$\begin{array}{r} 11 \\ \times\ 11 \\ \hline \end{array}$$

17)
$$\begin{array}{r} 11 \\ \times\ 8 \\ \hline \end{array}$$

18)
$$\begin{array}{r} 5 \\ \times\ 11 \\ \hline \end{array}$$

19)
$$\begin{array}{r} 11 \\ \times\ 6 \\ \hline \end{array}$$

20)
$$\begin{array}{r} 4 \\ \times\ 11 \\ \hline \end{array}$$

21)
$$\begin{array}{r} 11 \\ \times\ 9 \\ \hline \end{array}$$

22)
$$\begin{array}{r} 5 \\ \times\ 11 \\ \hline \end{array}$$

23)
$$\begin{array}{r} 11 \\ \times\ 11 \\ \hline \end{array}$$

24)
$$\begin{array}{r} 11 \\ \times\ 11 \\ \hline \end{array}$$

25)
$$\begin{array}{r} 11 \\ \times\ 8 \\ \hline \end{array}$$

26)
$$\begin{array}{r} 12 \\ \times\ 11 \\ \hline \end{array}$$

27)
$$\begin{array}{r} 11 \\ \times\ 9 \\ \hline \end{array}$$

28)
$$\begin{array}{r} 7 \\ \times\ 11 \\ \hline \end{array}$$

29)
$$\begin{array}{r} 11 \\ \times\ 10 \\ \hline \end{array}$$

30)
$$\begin{array}{r} 5 \\ \times\ 11 \\ \hline \end{array}$$

31)
$$\begin{array}{r} 11 \\ \times\ 2 \\ \hline \end{array}$$

32)
$$\begin{array}{r} 3 \\ \times\ 11 \\ \hline \end{array}$$

33)
$$\begin{array}{r} 11 \\ \times\ 7 \\ \hline \end{array}$$

34)
$$\begin{array}{r} 7 \\ \times\ 11 \\ \hline \end{array}$$

35)
$$\begin{array}{r} 11 \\ \times\ 1 \\ \hline \end{array}$$

36)
$$\begin{array}{r} 9 \\ \times\ 11 \\ \hline \end{array}$$

37)
$$\begin{array}{r} 11 \\ \times\ 3 \\ \hline \end{array}$$

38)
$$\begin{array}{r} 9 \\ \times\ 11 \\ \hline \end{array}$$

39)
$$\begin{array}{r} 11 \\ \times\ 12 \\ \hline \end{array}$$

40)
$$\begin{array}{r} 10 \\ \times\ 11 \\ \hline \end{array}$$

41)
$$\begin{array}{r} 11 \\ \times\ 12 \\ \hline \end{array}$$

42)
$$\begin{array}{r} 3 \\ \times\ 11 \\ \hline \end{array}$$

43)
$$\begin{array}{r} 11 \\ \times\ 0 \\ \hline \end{array}$$

44)
$$\begin{array}{r} 11 \\ \times\ 11 \\ \hline \end{array}$$

45)
$$\begin{array}{r} 11 \\ \times\ 1 \\ \hline \end{array}$$

46)
$$\begin{array}{r} 1 \\ \times\ 11 \\ \hline \end{array}$$

47)
$$\begin{array}{r} 11 \\ \times\ 11 \\ \hline \end{array}$$

48)
$$\begin{array}{r} 4 \\ \times\ 11 \\ \hline \end{array}$$

49)
$$\begin{array}{r} 11 \\ \times\ 4 \\ \hline \end{array}$$

50)
$$\begin{array}{r} 11 \\ \times\ 11 \\ \hline \end{array}$$

51)
$$\begin{array}{r} 11 \\ \times\ 6 \\ \hline \end{array}$$

52)
$$\begin{array}{r} 4 \\ \times\ 11 \\ \hline \end{array}$$

53)
$$\begin{array}{r} 11 \\ \times\ 11 \\ \hline \end{array}$$

54)
$$\begin{array}{r} 4 \\ \times\ 11 \\ \hline \end{array}$$

55)
$$\begin{array}{r} 11 \\ \times\ 1 \\ \hline \end{array}$$

56)
$$\begin{array}{r} 11 \\ \times\ 11 \\ \hline \end{array}$$

57)
$$\begin{array}{r} 11 \\ \times\ 11 \\ \hline \end{array}$$

58)
$$\begin{array}{r} 3 \\ \times\ 11 \\ \hline \end{array}$$

59)
$$\begin{array}{r} 11 \\ \times\ 1 \\ \hline \end{array}$$

60)
$$\begin{array}{r} 11 \\ \times\ 11 \\ \hline \end{array}$$

Time
:

Score
/60

DAY 75
· Multiplying 11 ·

1)　　　11　　　2)　　　　2　　　3)　　　11　　　4)　　　　8　　　5)　　　11　　　6)　　　　7　　　7)　　　11
　　×　12　　　　　×　11　　　　　×　 7　　　　　×　11　　　　　×　10　　　　　×　11　　　　　×　11

8)　　　12　　　9)　　　11　　10)　　　11　　11)　　　11　　12)　　　　7　　13)　　　11　　14)　　　　8
　　×　11　　　　　×　 8　　　　　×　11　　　　　×　 4　　　　　×　11　　　　　×　 3　　　　　×　11

15)　　　11　　16)　　　　5　　17)　　　11　　18)　　　　2　　19)　　　11　　20)　　　11　　21)　　　11
　　×　 4　　　　　×　11　　　　　×　 3　　　　　×　11　　　　　×　11　　　　　×　11　　　　　×　12

22)　　　　7　　23)　　　11　　24)　　　　2　　25)　　　11　　26)　　　11　　27)　　　11　　28)　　　　9
　　×　11　　　　　×　 8　　　　　×　11　　　　　×　 2　　　　　×　11　　　　　×　 8　　　　　×　11

29)　　　11　　30)　　　　9　　31)　　　11　　32)　　　11　　33)　　　11　　34)　　　　8　　35)　　　11
　　×　 7　　　　　×　11　　　　　×　 6　　　　　×　11　　　　　×　 6　　　　　×　11　　　　　×　 3

36)　　　　4　　37)　　　11　　38)　　　　5　　39)　　　11　　40)　　　　3　　41)　　　11　　42)　　　　5
　　×　11　　　　　×　 4　　　　　×　11　　　　　×　 7　　　　　×　11　　　　　×　 6　　　　　×　11

43)　　　11　　44)　　　　2　　45)　　　11　　46)　　　10　　47)　　　11　　48)　　　11　　49)　　　11
　　×　 7　　　　　×　11　　　　　×　 8　　　　　×　11　　　　　×　11　　　　　×　11　　　　　×　 5

50)　　　　5　　51)　　　11　　52)　　　　6　　53)　　　11　　54)　　　11　　55)　　　11　　56)　　　10
　　×　11　　　　　×　12　　　　　×　11　　　　　×　10　　　　　×　11　　　　　×　 8　　　　　×　11

57)　　　11　　58)　　　　3　　59)　　　11　　60)　　　　8
　　×　12　　　　　×　11　　　　　×　10　　　　　×　11

Time
:

Score
/60

HOW ABOUT WE GO WAY BACK IN TIME TO THE ANCIENT CIVILIZATION OF THE BABYLONIANS?

Their mathematicians are thought to have been the first ones to invent multiplication tables over 4000 years ago! Clay tablets that have survived from that era support the claim too.

As the Babylonian civilization grew bigger, they needed calculations to run an orderly and fair system. This became the multiplication table, similar to what we're using today!

DAY 76
· Multiplying 12 ·

1) 12 × 0

2) 8 × 12

3) 12 × 5

4) 4 × 12

5) 12 × 7

6) 8 × 12

7) 12 × 5

8) 5 × 12

9) 12 × 8

10) 9 × 12

11) 12 × 0

12) 4 × 12

13) 12 × 7

14) 4 × 12

15) 12 × 2

16) 7 × 12

17) 12 × 1

18) 0 × 12

19) 12 × 8

20) 4 × 12

21) 12 × 8

22) 1 × 12

23) 12 × 5

24) 7 × 12

25) 12 × 6

26) 3 × 12

27) 12 × 5

28) 6 × 12

29) 12 × 5

30) 2 × 12

31) 12 × 8

32) 3 × 12

33) 12 × 5

34) 7 × 12

35) 12 × 8

36) 3 × 12

37) 12 × 4

38) 6 × 12

39) 12 × 2

40) 0 × 12

41) 12 × 2

42) 9 × 12

43) 12 × 2

44) 7 × 12

45) 12 × 2

46) 5 × 12

47) 12 × 6

48) 9 × 12

49) 12 × 5

50) 1 × 12

51) 12 × 1

52) 6 × 12

53) 12 × 4

54) 4 × 12

55) 12 × 2

56) 2 × 12

57) 12 × 4

58) 5 × 12

59) 12 × 1

60) 1 × 12

Time :

Score

/60

DAY 77

· Multiplying 12 ·

1) 12 × 2

2) 8 × 12

3) 12 × 9

4) 6 × 12

5) 12 × 9

6) 5 × 12

7) 12 × 8

8) 7 × 12

9) 12 × 9

10) 9 × 12

11) 12 × 6

12) 5 × 12

13) 12 × 8

14) 9 × 12

15) 12 × 4

16) 4 × 12

17) 12 × 5

18) 8 × 12

19) 12 × 9

20) 9 × 12

21) 12 × 6

22) 7 × 12

23) 12 × 9

24) 4 × 12

25) 12 × 3

26) 4 × 12

27) 12 × 2

28) 6 × 12

29) 12 × 7

30) 2 × 12

31) 12 × 9

32) 7 × 12

33) 12 × 4

34) 6 × 12

35) 12 × 8

36) 8 × 12

37) 12 × 7

38) 3 × 12

39) 12 × 5

40) 9 × 12

41) 12 × 8

42) 9 × 12

43) 12 × 6

44) 3 × 12

45) 12 × 2

46) 6 × 12

47) 12 × 2

48) 9 × 12

49) 12 × 9

50) 9 × 12

51) 12 × 4

52) 2 × 12

53) 12 × 9

54) 5 × 12

55) 12 × 7

56) 6 × 12

57) 12 × 4

58) 9 × 12

59) 12 × 3

60) 6 × 12

Time :

Score /60

DAY 78
· Multiplying 12 ·

1) 12
  × 7

2)   6
  × 12

3) 12
  × 7

4)   9
  × 12

5) 12
  × 3

6)   7
  × 12

7) 12
  × 9

8)   7
  × 12

9) 12
  × 6

10) 2
  × 12

11) 12
  × 4

12) 9
  × 12

13) 12
  × 6

14) 2
  × 12

15) 12
  × 6

16) 9
  × 12

17) 12
  × 7

18) 9
  × 12

19) 12
  × 7

20) 4
  × 12

21) 12
  × 5

22) 4
  × 12

23) 12
  × 8

24) 3
  × 12

25) 12
  × 8

26) 2
  × 12

27) 12
  × 9

28) 5
  × 12

29) 12
  × 9

30) 3
  × 12

31) 12
  × 5

32) 3
  × 12

33) 12
  × 6

34) 5
  × 12

35) 12
  × 2

36) 5
  × 12

37) 12
  × 3

38) 6
  × 12

39) 12
  × 4

40) 7
  × 12

41) 12
  × 4

42) 9
  × 12

43) 12
  × 3

44) 6
  × 12

45) 12
  × 9

46) 6
  × 12

47) 12
  × 9

48) 4
  × 12

49) 12
  × 4

50) 2
  × 12

51) 12
  × 3

52) 6
  × 12

53) 12
  × 8

54) 4
  × 12

55) 12
  × 3

56) 8
  × 12

57) 12
  × 2

58) 2
  × 12

59) 12
  × 7

60) 4
  × 12

Time :

Score /60

DAY 79
· Multiplying 12 ·

1) 12 × 9

2) 3 × 12

3) 12 × 2

4) 7 × 12

5) 12 × 9

6) 9 × 12

7) 12 × 8

8) 8 × 12

9) 12 × 5

10) 9 × 12

11) 12 × 9

12) 5 × 12

13) 12 × 2

14) 8 × 12

15) 12 × 2

16) 5 × 12

17) 12 × 7

18) 7 × 12

19) 12 × 4

20) 9 × 12

21) 12 × 8

22) 7 × 12

23) 12 × 8

24) 9 × 12

25) 12 × 8

26) 8 × 12

27) 12 × 7

28) 6 × 12

29) 12 × 9

30) 5 × 12

31) 12 × 5

32) 8 × 12

33) 12 × 9

34) 5 × 12

35) 12 × 4

36) 7 × 12

37) 12 × 9

38) 8 × 12

39) 12 × 3

40) 5 × 12

41) 12 × 9

42) 7 × 12

43) 12 × 2

44) 8 × 12

45) 12 × 5

46) 6 × 12

47) 12 × 8

48) 2 × 12

49) 12 × 9

50) 2 × 12

51) 12 × 4

52) 8 × 12

53) 12 × 8

54) 7 × 12

55) 12 × 6

56) 6 × 12

57) 12 × 9

58) 9 × 12

59) 12 × 3

60) 6 × 12

Time :

Score /60

DAY 80
· Multiplying 12 ·

1)　　12　　2)　　　9　　3)　　12　　4)　　　6　　5)　　12　　6)　　　9　　7)　　12
　　×　10　　　　×　12　　　×　　3　　　×　12　　　×　11　　　×　12　　　×　　5

8)　　　8　　9)　　12　　10)　　10　　11)　　12　　12)　　　5　　13)　　12　　14)　　　3
　　×　12　　　×　　7　　　×　12　　　×　　3　　　×　12　　　×　10　　　×　12

15)　　12　　16)　　　3　　17)　　12　　18)　　　6　　19)　　12　　20)　　　3　　21)　　12
　　×　　6　　　×　12　　　×　　5　　　×　12　　　×　　4　　　×　12　　　×　　6

22)　　10　　23)　　12　　24)　　　7　　25)　　12　　26)　　　7　　27)　　12　　28)　　　5
　　×　12　　　×　11　　　×　12　　　×　　4　　　×　12　　　×　　3　　　×　12

29)　　12　　30)　　　4　　31)　　12　　32)　　10　　33)　　12　　34)　　　4　　35)　　12
　　×　　2　　　×　12　　　×　　5　　　×　12　　　×　　9　　　×　12　　　×　10

36)　　　9　　37)　　12　　38)　　　3　　39)　　12　　40)　　　3　　41)　　12　　42)　　　2
　　×　12　　　×　　3　　　×　12　　　×　　2　　　×　12　　　×　11　　　×　12

43)　　12　　44)　　　2　　45)　　12　　46)　　　9　　47)　　12　　48)　　　9　　49)　　12
　　×　　4　　　×　12　　　×　　2　　　×　12　　　×　　6　　　×　12　　　×　11

50)　　　4　　51)　　12　　52)　　　8　　53)　　12　　54)　　　5　　55)　　12　　56)　　　6
　　×　12　　　×　　7　　　×　12　　　×　　4　　　×　12　　　×　　8　　　×　12

57)　　12　　58)　　　7　　59)　　12　　60)　　10
　　×　　2　　　×　12　　　×　　4　　　×　12

Time
:

Score

/60

DAY 81
· Multiplying 12 ·

1)
```
   12
×  12
```

2)
```
    7
×  12
```

3)
```
   12
×   3
```

4)
```
    0
×  12
```

5)
```
   12
×   5
```

6)
```
   12
×  12
```

7)
```
   12
×   4
```

8)
```
    7
×  12
```

9)
```
   12
×   6
```

10)
```
   10
×  12
```

11)
```
   12
×   1
```

12)
```
    6
×  12
```

13)
```
   12
×   5
```

14)
```
    1
×  12
```

15)
```
   12
×   5
```

16)
```
    5
×  12
```

17)
```
   12
×   8
```

18)
```
    1
×  12
```

19)
```
   12
×   4
```

20)
```
    6
×  12
```

21)
```
   12
×   0
```

22)
```
   10
×  12
```

23)
```
   12
×   5
```

24)
```
    4
×  12
```

25)
```
   12
×   8
```

26)
```
   12
×  12
```

27)
```
   12
×   1
```

28)
```
    0
×  12
```

29)
```
   12
×  11
```

30)
```
   11
×  12
```

31)
```
   12
×   6
```

32)
```
    2
×  12
```

33)
```
   12
×   5
```

34)
```
   11
×  12
```

35)
```
   12
×   9
```

36)
```
    1
×  12
```

37)
```
   12
×   2
```

38)
```
    2
×  12
```

39)
```
   12
×   3
```

40)
```
   10
×  12
```

41)
```
   12
×   5
```

42)
```
   11
×  12
```

43)
```
   12
×   3
```

44)
```
    3
×  12
```

45)
```
   12
×   9
```

46)
```
    3
×  12
```

47)
```
   12
×  12
```

48)
```
    3
×  12
```

49)
```
   12
×   7
```

50)
```
    5
×  12
```

51)
```
   12
×   1
```

52)
```
    0
×  12
```

53)
```
   12
×   2
```

54)
```
    0
×  12
```

55)
```
   12
×   1
```

56)
```
    6
×  12
```

57)
```
   12
×  11
```

58)
```
    1
×  12
```

59)
```
   12
×  10
```

60)
```
    8
×  12
```

Time
:

Score
/60

DAY 82
· Multiplying 12 ·

1) 12 × 11
2) 4 × 12
3) 12 × 12
4) 11 × 12
5) 12 × 2
6) 8 × 12
7) 12 × 11

8) 10 × 12
9) 12 × 4
10) 7 × 12
11) 12 × 11
12) 5 × 12
13) 12 × 7
14) 8 × 12

15) 12 × 7
16) 5 × 12
17) 12 × 5
18) 10 × 12
19) 12 × 6
20) 6 × 12
21) 12 × 8

22) 4 × 12
23) 12 × 8
24) 11 × 12
25) 12 × 5
26) 11 × 12
27) 12 × 6
28) 10 × 12

29) 12 × 12
30) 2 × 12
31) 12 × 7
32) 3 × 12
33) 12 × 11
34) 12 × 12
35) 12 × 10

36) 10 × 12
37) 12 × 9
38) 6 × 12
39) 12 × 8
40) 8 × 12
41) 12 × 12
42) 7 × 12

43) 12 × 9
44) 10 × 12
45) 12 × 5
46) 3 × 12
47) 12 × 9
48) 10 × 12
49) 12 × 5

50) 8 × 12
51) 12 × 12
52) 12 × 12
53) 12 × 8
54) 9 × 12
55) 12 × 6
56) 9 × 12

57) 12 × 11
58) 5 × 12
59) 12 × 5
60) 8 × 12

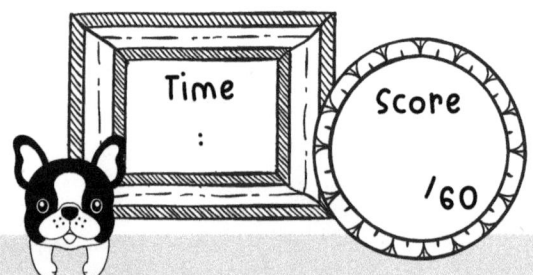

Time :

Score /60

DAY 83
· Multiplying 12 ·

1) 12 × 7
2) 9 × 12
3) 12 × 9
4) 4 × 12
5) 12 × 8
6) 5 × 12
7) 12 × 3

8) 6 × 12
9) 12 × 2
10) 4 × 12
11) 12 × 4
12) 7 × 12
13) 12 × 12
14) 8 × 12

15) 12 × 9
16) 9 × 12
17) 12 × 2
18) 12 × 12
19) 12 × 10
20) 10 × 12
21) 12 × 12

22) 2 × 12
23) 12 × 3
24) 2 × 12
25) 12 × 6
26) 5 × 12
27) 12 × 7
28) 6 × 12

29) 12 × 12
30) 2 × 12
31) 12 × 12
32) 9 × 12
33) 12 × 9
34) 11 × 12
35) 12 × 12

36) 4 × 12
37) 12 × 4
38) 7 × 12
39) 12 × 3
40) 2 × 12
41) 12 × 11
42) 4 × 12

43) 12 × 7
44) 8 × 12
45) 12 × 8
46) 5 × 12
47) 12 × 4
48) 10 × 12
49) 12 × 4

50) 12 × 12
51) 12 × 6
52) 8 × 12
53) 12 × 4
54) 5 × 12
55) 12 × 12
56) 4 × 12

57) 12 × 7
58) 7 × 12
59) 12 × 7
60) 8 × 12

Time :

Score /60

POP QUIZ!

There are 2 day-to-day ways of measuring temperature: Celsius, and Fahrenheit, but what is the only temperature that is the same for both?

-40, that's absolutely freezing no matter how you look at it!

There are many countries around the world that can get down to temperatures like this in winter, I think my paws would freeze right off. On the other hand (or paw!), frozen bananas can be a delicious treat on a hot summer day.

DAY 84
· Mixed Questions ·

1) 6 × 2

2) 12 × 5

3) 3 × 2

4) 8 × 5

5) 4 × 2

6) 10 × 9

7) 11 × 6

8) 5 × 10

9) 9 × 5

10) 7 × 10

11) 9 × 4

12) 12 × 12

13) 7 × 8

14) 7 × 10

15) 11 × 5

16) 8 × 9

17) 12 × 7

18) 10 × 3

19) 5 × 10

20) 11 × 5

21) 4 × 2

22) 12 × 7

23) 6 × 2

24) 3 × 6

25) 8 × 10

26) 5 × 12

27) 7 × 11

28) 10 × 3

29) 11 × 7

30) 5 × 11

31) 3 × 4

32) 3 × 11

33) 7 × 4

34) 8 × 8

35) 2 × 8

36) 8 × 4

37) 7 × 2

38) 7 × 7

39) 11 × 5

40) 6 × 9

41) 4 × 6

42) 8 × 11

43) 7 × 7

44) 4 × 4

45) 10 × 5

46) 6 × 9

47) 12 × 10

48) 12 × 4

49) 6 × 8

50) 7 × 9

51) 5 × 10

52) 2 × 6

53) 2 × 9

54) 11 × 4

55) 12 × 5

56) 2 × 8

57) 12 × 12

58) 7 × 12

59) 11 × 10

60) 9 × 8

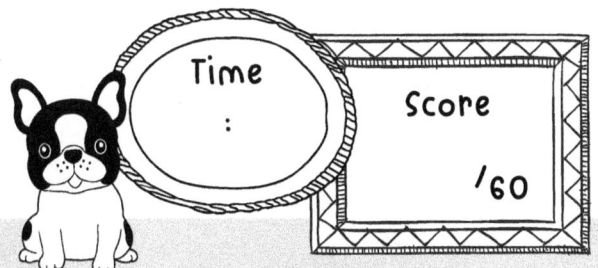

Time :

Score /60

DAY 85
· Mixed Questions ·

1) $\begin{array}{r} 3 \\ \times\ 11 \\ \hline \end{array}$ 2) $\begin{array}{r} 4 \\ \times\ 7 \\ \hline \end{array}$ 3) $\begin{array}{r} 9 \\ \times\ 8 \\ \hline \end{array}$ 4) $\begin{array}{r} 4 \\ \times\ 6 \\ \hline \end{array}$ 5) $\begin{array}{r} 3 \\ \times\ 10 \\ \hline \end{array}$ 6) $\begin{array}{r} 9 \\ \times\ 4 \\ \hline \end{array}$ 7) $\begin{array}{r} 8 \\ \times\ 11 \\ \hline \end{array}$

8) $\begin{array}{r} 2 \\ \times\ 4 \\ \hline \end{array}$ 9) $\begin{array}{r} 4 \\ \times\ 6 \\ \hline \end{array}$ 10) $\begin{array}{r} 4 \\ \times\ 6 \\ \hline \end{array}$ 11) $\begin{array}{r} 6 \\ \times\ 10 \\ \hline \end{array}$ 12) $\begin{array}{r} 2 \\ \times\ 11 \\ \hline \end{array}$ 13) $\begin{array}{r} 4 \\ \times\ 3 \\ \hline \end{array}$ 14) $\begin{array}{r} 3 \\ \times\ 3 \\ \hline \end{array}$

15) $\begin{array}{r} 9 \\ \times\ 8 \\ \hline \end{array}$ 16) $\begin{array}{r} 12 \\ \times\ 8 \\ \hline \end{array}$ 17) $\begin{array}{r} 2 \\ \times\ 7 \\ \hline \end{array}$ 18) $\begin{array}{r} 5 \\ \times\ 5 \\ \hline \end{array}$ 19) $\begin{array}{r} 8 \\ \times\ 4 \\ \hline \end{array}$ 20) $\begin{array}{r} 4 \\ \times\ 8 \\ \hline \end{array}$ 21) $\begin{array}{r} 11 \\ \times\ 11 \\ \hline \end{array}$

22) $\begin{array}{r} 6 \\ \times\ 10 \\ \hline \end{array}$ 23) $\begin{array}{r} 4 \\ \times\ 5 \\ \hline \end{array}$ 24) $\begin{array}{r} 6 \\ \times\ 9 \\ \hline \end{array}$ 25) $\begin{array}{r} 2 \\ \times\ 10 \\ \hline \end{array}$ 26) $\begin{array}{r} 3 \\ \times\ 7 \\ \hline \end{array}$ 27) $\begin{array}{r} 7 \\ \times\ 12 \\ \hline \end{array}$ 28) $\begin{array}{r} 10 \\ \times\ 11 \\ \hline \end{array}$

29) $\begin{array}{r} 7 \\ \times\ 12 \\ \hline \end{array}$ 30) $\begin{array}{r} 5 \\ \times\ 11 \\ \hline \end{array}$ 31) $\begin{array}{r} 6 \\ \times\ 9 \\ \hline \end{array}$ 32) $\begin{array}{r} 12 \\ \times\ 2 \\ \hline \end{array}$ 33) $\begin{array}{r} 11 \\ \times\ 2 \\ \hline \end{array}$ 34) $\begin{array}{r} 6 \\ \times\ 3 \\ \hline \end{array}$ 35) $\begin{array}{r} 10 \\ \times\ 10 \\ \hline \end{array}$

36) $\begin{array}{r} 10 \\ \times\ 12 \\ \hline \end{array}$ 37) $\begin{array}{r} 3 \\ \times\ 2 \\ \hline \end{array}$ 38) $\begin{array}{r} 4 \\ \times\ 2 \\ \hline \end{array}$ 39) $\begin{array}{r} 9 \\ \times\ 4 \\ \hline \end{array}$ 40) $\begin{array}{r} 7 \\ \times\ 12 \\ \hline \end{array}$ 41) $\begin{array}{r} 5 \\ \times\ 12 \\ \hline \end{array}$ 42) $\begin{array}{r} 4 \\ \times\ 10 \\ \hline \end{array}$

43) $\begin{array}{r} 7 \\ \times\ 3 \\ \hline \end{array}$ 44) $\begin{array}{r} 4 \\ \times\ 10 \\ \hline \end{array}$ 45) $\begin{array}{r} 6 \\ \times\ 6 \\ \hline \end{array}$ 46) $\begin{array}{r} 3 \\ \times\ 6 \\ \hline \end{array}$ 47) $\begin{array}{r} 5 \\ \times\ 2 \\ \hline \end{array}$ 48) $\begin{array}{r} 7 \\ \times\ 10 \\ \hline \end{array}$ 49) $\begin{array}{r} 9 \\ \times\ 2 \\ \hline \end{array}$

50) $\begin{array}{r} 11 \\ \times\ 10 \\ \hline \end{array}$ 51) $\begin{array}{r} 3 \\ \times\ 8 \\ \hline \end{array}$ 52) $\begin{array}{r} 9 \\ \times\ 11 \\ \hline \end{array}$ 53) $\begin{array}{r} 10 \\ \times\ 9 \\ \hline \end{array}$ 54) $\begin{array}{r} 12 \\ \times\ 9 \\ \hline \end{array}$ 55) $\begin{array}{r} 12 \\ \times\ 7 \\ \hline \end{array}$ 56) $\begin{array}{r} 8 \\ \times\ 2 \\ \hline \end{array}$

57) $\begin{array}{r} 10 \\ \times\ 9 \\ \hline \end{array}$ 58) $\begin{array}{r} 4 \\ \times\ 4 \\ \hline \end{array}$ 59) $\begin{array}{r} 2 \\ \times\ 4 \\ \hline \end{array}$ 60) $\begin{array}{r} 9 \\ \times\ 3 \\ \hline \end{array}$

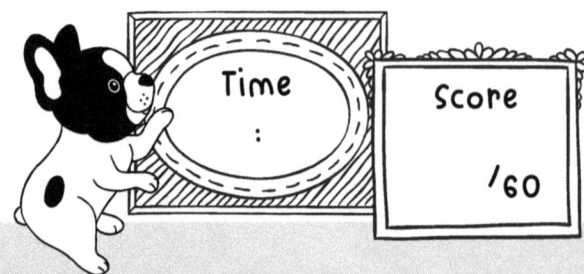

Time
:

Score

/60

DAY 86
· Mixed Questions ·

1) 11 × 12
2) 11 × 5
3) 6 × 11
4) 7 × 11
5) 11 × 9
6) 8 × 11
7) 12 × 7

8) 8 × 4
9) 3 × 5
10) 8 × 8
11) 2 × 8
12) 6 × 12
13) 6 × 5
14) 11 × 4

15) 8 × 2
16) 10 × 6
17) 2 × 11
18) 9 × 7
19) 12 × 10
20) 7 × 11
21) 6 × 10

22) 6 × 6
23) 11 × 6
24) 6 × 7
25) 6 × 11
26) 11 × 2
27) 10 × 11
28) 4 × 6

29) 4 × 10
30) 7 × 5
31) 8 × 5
32) 7 × 4
33) 2 × 8
34) 9 × 12
35) 6 × 10

36) 6 × 6
37) 5 × 9
38) 4 × 8
39) 7 × 7
40) 5 × 5
41) 3 × 8
42) 9 × 11

43) 4 × 5
44) 12 × 8
45) 6 × 8
46) 11 × 3
47) 9 × 7
48) 11 × 11
49) 4 × 10

50) 4 × 4
51) 8 × 7
52) 2 × 6
53) 3 × 2
54) 6 × 11
55) 9 × 6
56) 3 × 2

57) 10 × 10
58) 9 × 3
59) 4 × 12
60) 6 × 10

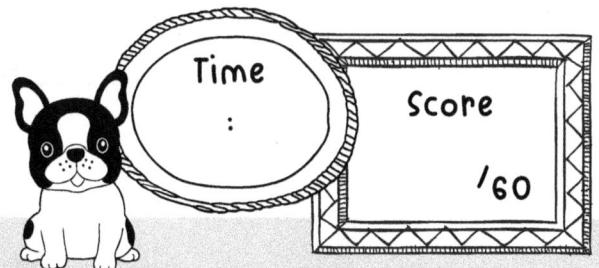

Time :

Score /60

DAY 87
· Mixed Questions ·

1)   4
 × 12

2)   6
 × 4

3)   9
 × 10

4)   11
 × 2

5)   2
 × 7

6)   9
 × 11

7)   2
 × 12

8)   7
 × 8

9)   12
 × 6

10)   9
 × 7

11)   10
 × 10

12)   9
 × 5

13)   7
 × 4

14)   11
 × 11

15)   4
 × 11

16)   2
 × 7

17)   6
 × 6

18)   2
 × 9

19)   3
 × 4

20)   3
 × 7

21)   5
 × 11

22)   3
 × 4

23)   6
 × 11

24)   2
 × 2

25)   4
 × 3

26)   5
 × 11

27)   5
 × 5

28)   7
 × 11

29)   12
 × 12

30)   11
 × 7

31)   4
 × 6

32)   5
 × 6

33)   11
 × 4

34)   5
 × 3

35)   6
 × 3

36)   6
 × 12

37)   10
 × 9

38)   7
 × 2

39)   9
 × 8

40)   4
 × 9

41)   7
 × 8

42)   9
 × 6

43)   11
 × 2

44)   6
 × 6

45)   7
 × 6

46)   10
 × 5

47)   2
 × 8

48)   7
 × 5

49)   12
 × 11

50)   4
 × 11

51)   5
 × 9

52)   8
 × 5

53)   4
 × 5

54)   7
 × 11

55)   9
 × 4

56)   8
 × 2

57)   8
 × 11

58)   8
 × 9

59)   8
 × 4

60)   11
 × 10

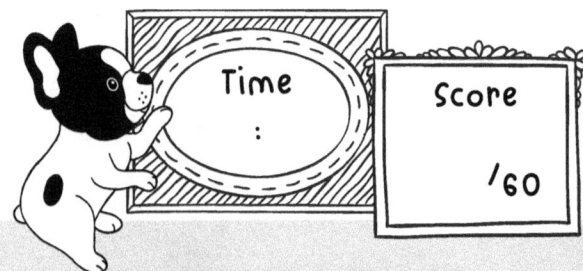

Time
:

Score

/60

DAY 88
· Mixed Questions ·

1)   11
  ×   7

2)   4
  ×   6

3)   6
  ×   0

4)   2
  ×   8

5)   7
  ×   1

6)   8
  ×   3

7)   4
  × 10

8)   6
  ×   6

9)   6
  ×   8

10)   12
  ×   9

11)   11
  ×   5

12)   0
  ×   3

13)   8
  ×   1

14)   4
  × 10

15)   2
  × 12

16)   1
  ×   5

17)   3
  ×   5

18)   6
  ×   5

19)   7
  × 10

20)   9
  ×   8

21)   5
  ×   0

22)   4
  ×   9

23)   9
  × 11

24)   6
  ×   2

25)   6
  ×   4

26)   2
  × 10

27)   10
  ×   2

28)   9
  ×   4

29)   12
  × 10

30)   0
  ×   5

31)   4
  ×   0

32)   3
  × 12

33)   4
  ×   7

34)   7
  ×   4

35)   12
  ×   2

36)   7
  ×   4

37)   3
  × 12

38)   9
  ×   4

39)   4
  ×   9

40)   0
  ×   7

41)   5
  ×   2

42)   1
  ×   9

43)   9
  × 12

44)   8
  × 11

45)   12
  ×   0

46)   1
  ×   7

47)   8
  ×   5

48)   6
  ×   6

49)   11
  ×   2

50)   4
  ×   8

51)   12
  × 12

52)   12
  × 12

53)   7
  ×   8

54)   7
  × 10

55)   5
  ×   3

56)   0
  × 12

57)   6
  ×   5

58)   12
  ×   4

59)   7
  ×   7

60)   8
  ×   2

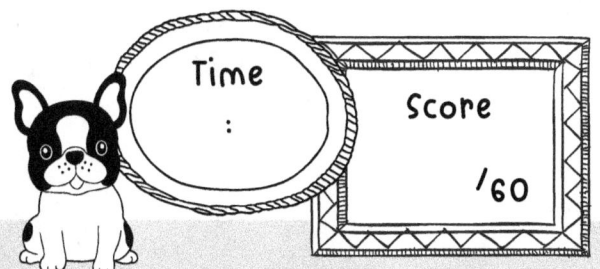

Time :

Score

/60

DAY 89
· Mixed Questions ·

1)
$$\begin{array}{r} 10 \\ \times\ 8 \\ \hline \end{array}$$

2)
$$\begin{array}{r} 2 \\ \times\ 6 \\ \hline \end{array}$$

3)
$$\begin{array}{r} 5 \\ \times\ 6 \\ \hline \end{array}$$

4)
$$\begin{array}{r} 4 \\ \times\ 3 \\ \hline \end{array}$$

5)
$$\begin{array}{r} 9 \\ \times\ 7 \\ \hline \end{array}$$

6)
$$\begin{array}{r} 8 \\ \times\ 7 \\ \hline \end{array}$$

7)
$$\begin{array}{r} 7 \\ \times\ 6 \\ \hline \end{array}$$

8)
$$\begin{array}{r} 12 \\ \times\ 4 \\ \hline \end{array}$$

9)
$$\begin{array}{r} 5 \\ \times\ 3 \\ \hline \end{array}$$

10)
$$\begin{array}{r} 9 \\ \times\ 12 \\ \hline \end{array}$$

11)
$$\begin{array}{r} 4 \\ \times\ 2 \\ \hline \end{array}$$

12)
$$\begin{array}{r} 4 \\ \times\ 4 \\ \hline \end{array}$$

13)
$$\begin{array}{r} 12 \\ \times\ 12 \\ \hline \end{array}$$

14)
$$\begin{array}{r} 12 \\ \times\ 11 \\ \hline \end{array}$$

15)
$$\begin{array}{r} 12 \\ \times\ 2 \\ \hline \end{array}$$

16)
$$\begin{array}{r} 10 \\ \times\ 11 \\ \hline \end{array}$$

17)
$$\begin{array}{r} 5 \\ \times\ 8 \\ \hline \end{array}$$

18)
$$\begin{array}{r} 5 \\ \times\ 3 \\ \hline \end{array}$$

19)
$$\begin{array}{r} 5 \\ \times\ 7 \\ \hline \end{array}$$

20)
$$\begin{array}{r} 12 \\ \times\ 7 \\ \hline \end{array}$$

21)
$$\begin{array}{r} 4 \\ \times\ 8 \\ \hline \end{array}$$

22)
$$\begin{array}{r} 11 \\ \times\ 2 \\ \hline \end{array}$$

23)
$$\begin{array}{r} 3 \\ \times\ 12 \\ \hline \end{array}$$

24)
$$\begin{array}{r} 4 \\ \times\ 3 \\ \hline \end{array}$$

25)
$$\begin{array}{r} 7 \\ \times\ 9 \\ \hline \end{array}$$

26)
$$\begin{array}{r} 12 \\ \times\ 3 \\ \hline \end{array}$$

27)
$$\begin{array}{r} 3 \\ \times\ 8 \\ \hline \end{array}$$

28)
$$\begin{array}{r} 2 \\ \times\ 6 \\ \hline \end{array}$$

29)
$$\begin{array}{r} 2 \\ \times\ 11 \\ \hline \end{array}$$

30)
$$\begin{array}{r} 10 \\ \times\ 8 \\ \hline \end{array}$$

31)
$$\begin{array}{r} 2 \\ \times\ 6 \\ \hline \end{array}$$

32)
$$\begin{array}{r} 4 \\ \times\ 2 \\ \hline \end{array}$$

33)
$$\begin{array}{r} 6 \\ \times\ 8 \\ \hline \end{array}$$

34)
$$\begin{array}{r} 4 \\ \times\ 3 \\ \hline \end{array}$$

35)
$$\begin{array}{r} 5 \\ \times\ 7 \\ \hline \end{array}$$

36)
$$\begin{array}{r} 2 \\ \times\ 5 \\ \hline \end{array}$$

37)
$$\begin{array}{r} 12 \\ \times\ 2 \\ \hline \end{array}$$

38)
$$\begin{array}{r} 6 \\ \times\ 12 \\ \hline \end{array}$$

39)
$$\begin{array}{r} 7 \\ \times\ 2 \\ \hline \end{array}$$

40)
$$\begin{array}{r} 10 \\ \times\ 3 \\ \hline \end{array}$$

41)
$$\begin{array}{r} 3 \\ \times\ 12 \\ \hline \end{array}$$

42)
$$\begin{array}{r} 7 \\ \times\ 6 \\ \hline \end{array}$$

43)
$$\begin{array}{r} 5 \\ \times\ 4 \\ \hline \end{array}$$

44)
$$\begin{array}{r} 10 \\ \times\ 7 \\ \hline \end{array}$$

45)
$$\begin{array}{r} 6 \\ \times\ 4 \\ \hline \end{array}$$

46)
$$\begin{array}{r} 2 \\ \times\ 8 \\ \hline \end{array}$$

47)
$$\begin{array}{r} 4 \\ \times\ 10 \\ \hline \end{array}$$

48)
$$\begin{array}{r} 4 \\ \times\ 4 \\ \hline \end{array}$$

49)
$$\begin{array}{r} 9 \\ \times\ 2 \\ \hline \end{array}$$

50)
$$\begin{array}{r} 2 \\ \times\ 12 \\ \hline \end{array}$$

51)
$$\begin{array}{r} 5 \\ \times\ 7 \\ \hline \end{array}$$

52)
$$\begin{array}{r} 2 \\ \times\ 4 \\ \hline \end{array}$$

53)
$$\begin{array}{r} 6 \\ \times\ 4 \\ \hline \end{array}$$

54)
$$\begin{array}{r} 8 \\ \times\ 4 \\ \hline \end{array}$$

55)
$$\begin{array}{r} 12 \\ \times\ 4 \\ \hline \end{array}$$

56)
$$\begin{array}{r} 6 \\ \times\ 12 \\ \hline \end{array}$$

57)
$$\begin{array}{r} 2 \\ \times\ 2 \\ \hline \end{array}$$

58)
$$\begin{array}{r} 9 \\ \times\ 11 \\ \hline \end{array}$$

59)
$$\begin{array}{r} 4 \\ \times\ 11 \\ \hline \end{array}$$

60)
$$\begin{array}{r} 11 \\ \times\ 4 \\ \hline \end{array}$$

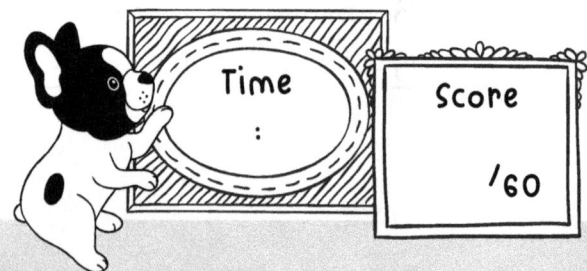

Time
:

Score

/60

DAY 90
· Mixed Questions ·

1) 11
   × 9

2)   2
   × 9

3) 10
   × 11

4)   8
   × 2

5)   5
   × 6

6) 12
   × 7

7)   7
   × 4

8) 11
   × 2

9)   6
   × 12

10)   2
    × 6

11) 10
   × 5

12)   6
   × 11

13)   8
   × 3

14) 10
   × 3

15) 10
   × 10

16) 12
   × 7

17) 10
   × 4

18)   8
   × 2

19)   3
   × 2

20) 11
   × 12

21)   6
   × 8

22)   4
   × 10

23)   4
   × 6

24)   9
   × 9

25) 12
   × 10

26) 12
   × 10

27)   3
   × 8

28) 11
   × 12

29)   2
   × 4

30)   8
   × 12

31)   5
   × 10

32)   7
   × 5

33) 10
   × 9

34)   4
   × 3

35)   2
   × 7

36)   6
   × 3

37)   3
   × 4

38)   9
   × 2

39)   6
   × 5

40)   4
   × 3

41)   5
   × 11

42) 12
   × 7

43) 11
   × 9

44) 12
   × 3

45)   9
   × 7

46)   5
   × 10

47)   5
   × 7

48)   7
   × 6

49) 10
   × 5

50)   3
   × 5

51) 11
   × 11

52)   7
   × 6

53)   2
   × 6

54) 11
   × 10

55)   9
   × 5

56)   4
   × 8

57) 12
   × 7

58)   6
   × 4

59)   8
   × 11

60)   4
   × 5

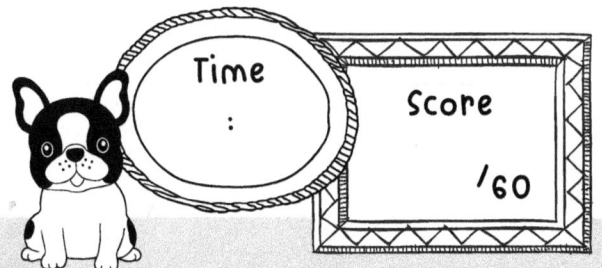

Time
:

Score

/60

DAY 91

· Mixed Questions ·

1) 12 × 3
2) 10 × 4
3) 5 × 12
4) 5 × 10
5) 9 × 10
6) 7 × 12
7) 2 × 11

8) 7 × 5
9) 12 × 10
10) 5 × 2
11) 12 × 12
12) 4 × 2
13) 3 × 12
14) 3 × 9

15) 12 × 11
16) 10 × 3
17) 3 × 6
18) 11 × 9
19) 10 × 8
20) 10 × 2
21) 6 × 8

22) 12 × 11
23) 9 × 9
24) 10 × 4
25) 4 × 9
26) 11 × 5
27) 9 × 10
28) 12 × 12

29) 11 × 3
30) 5 × 10
31) 11 × 2
32) 12 × 6
33) 11 × 4
34) 12 × 12
35) 12 × 3

36) 11 × 5
37) 4 × 7
38) 8 × 8
39) 5 × 3
40) 9 × 5
41) 6 × 4
42) 11 × 2

43) 10 × 5
44) 5 × 11
45) 4 × 3
46) 7 × 2
47) 5 × 10
48) 4 × 2
49) 10 × 12

50) 8 × 6
51) 8 × 4
52) 12 × 3
53) 12 × 2
54) 11 × 8
55) 10 × 9
56) 5 × 11

57) 7 × 3
58) 3 × 9
59) 9 × 2
60) 5 × 12

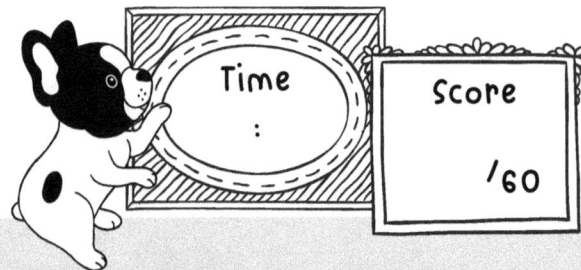

Time :

Score /60

DAY 92

· Mixed Questions ·

1) $\begin{array}{r} 11 \\ \times\ 7 \\ \hline \end{array}$
2) $\begin{array}{r} 6 \\ \times\ 7 \\ \hline \end{array}$
3) $\begin{array}{r} 5 \\ \times\ 10 \\ \hline \end{array}$
4) $\begin{array}{r} 6 \\ \times\ 5 \\ \hline \end{array}$
5) $\begin{array}{r} 3 \\ \times\ 6 \\ \hline \end{array}$
6) $\begin{array}{r} 9 \\ \times\ 10 \\ \hline \end{array}$
7) $\begin{array}{r} 10 \\ \times\ 11 \\ \hline \end{array}$

8) $\begin{array}{r} 6 \\ \times\ 6 \\ \hline \end{array}$
9) $\begin{array}{r} 12 \\ \times\ 5 \\ \hline \end{array}$
10) $\begin{array}{r} 12 \\ \times\ 12 \\ \hline \end{array}$
11) $\begin{array}{r} 9 \\ \times\ 7 \\ \hline \end{array}$
12) $\begin{array}{r} 7 \\ \times\ 9 \\ \hline \end{array}$
13) $\begin{array}{r} 8 \\ \times\ 4 \\ \hline \end{array}$
14) $\begin{array}{r} 3 \\ \times\ 10 \\ \hline \end{array}$

15) $\begin{array}{r} 7 \\ \times\ 12 \\ \hline \end{array}$
16) $\begin{array}{r} 7 \\ \times\ 3 \\ \hline \end{array}$
17) $\begin{array}{r} 11 \\ \times\ 6 \\ \hline \end{array}$
18) $\begin{array}{r} 8 \\ \times\ 5 \\ \hline \end{array}$
19) $\begin{array}{r} 7 \\ \times\ 8 \\ \hline \end{array}$
20) $\begin{array}{r} 3 \\ \times\ 7 \\ \hline \end{array}$
21) $\begin{array}{r} 10 \\ \times\ 9 \\ \hline \end{array}$

22) $\begin{array}{r} 5 \\ \times\ 12 \\ \hline \end{array}$
23) $\begin{array}{r} 9 \\ \times\ 3 \\ \hline \end{array}$
24) $\begin{array}{r} 5 \\ \times\ 10 \\ \hline \end{array}$
25) $\begin{array}{r} 5 \\ \times\ 9 \\ \hline \end{array}$
26) $\begin{array}{r} 10 \\ \times\ 6 \\ \hline \end{array}$
27) $\begin{array}{r} 9 \\ \times\ 2 \\ \hline \end{array}$
28) $\begin{array}{r} 5 \\ \times\ 9 \\ \hline \end{array}$

29) $\begin{array}{r} 9 \\ \times\ 8 \\ \hline \end{array}$
30) $\begin{array}{r} 12 \\ \times\ 5 \\ \hline \end{array}$
31) $\begin{array}{r} 9 \\ \times\ 7 \\ \hline \end{array}$
32) $\begin{array}{r} 11 \\ \times\ 5 \\ \hline \end{array}$
33) $\begin{array}{r} 10 \\ \times\ 3 \\ \hline \end{array}$
34) $\begin{array}{r} 4 \\ \times\ 10 \\ \hline \end{array}$
35) $\begin{array}{r} 7 \\ \times\ 9 \\ \hline \end{array}$

36) $\begin{array}{r} 12 \\ \times\ 3 \\ \hline \end{array}$
37) $\begin{array}{r} 7 \\ \times\ 7 \\ \hline \end{array}$
38) $\begin{array}{r} 3 \\ \times\ 6 \\ \hline \end{array}$
39) $\begin{array}{r} 4 \\ \times\ 7 \\ \hline \end{array}$
40) $\begin{array}{r} 4 \\ \times\ 8 \\ \hline \end{array}$
41) $\begin{array}{r} 8 \\ \times\ 3 \\ \hline \end{array}$
42) $\begin{array}{r} 3 \\ \times\ 12 \\ \hline \end{array}$

43) $\begin{array}{r} 6 \\ \times\ 9 \\ \hline \end{array}$
44) $\begin{array}{r} 10 \\ \times\ 10 \\ \hline \end{array}$
45) $\begin{array}{r} 7 \\ \times\ 5 \\ \hline \end{array}$
46) $\begin{array}{r} 9 \\ \times\ 5 \\ \hline \end{array}$
47) $\begin{array}{r} 8 \\ \times\ 7 \\ \hline \end{array}$
48) $\begin{array}{r} 7 \\ \times\ 11 \\ \hline \end{array}$
49) $\begin{array}{r} 5 \\ \times\ 4 \\ \hline \end{array}$

50) $\begin{array}{r} 11 \\ \times\ 6 \\ \hline \end{array}$
51) $\begin{array}{r} 4 \\ \times\ 8 \\ \hline \end{array}$
52) $\begin{array}{r} 10 \\ \times\ 9 \\ \hline \end{array}$
53) $\begin{array}{r} 9 \\ \times\ 6 \\ \hline \end{array}$
54) $\begin{array}{r} 11 \\ \times\ 8 \\ \hline \end{array}$
55) $\begin{array}{r} 5 \\ \times\ 7 \\ \hline \end{array}$
56) $\begin{array}{r} 11 \\ \times\ 5 \\ \hline \end{array}$

57) $\begin{array}{r} 3 \\ \times\ 8 \\ \hline \end{array}$
58) $\begin{array}{r} 11 \\ \times\ 12 \\ \hline \end{array}$
59) $\begin{array}{r} 2 \\ \times\ 9 \\ \hline \end{array}$
60) $\begin{array}{r} 5 \\ \times\ 12 \\ \hline \end{array}$

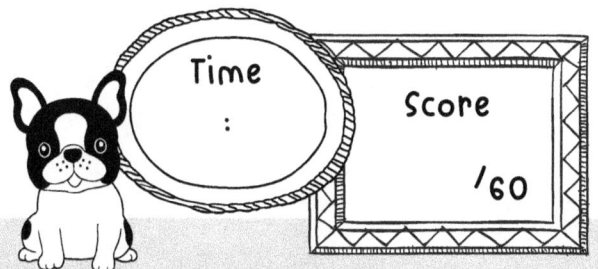

Time :

Score   /60

DAY 93
· Mixed Questions ·

1)　　3　2)　　12　3)　　3　4)　　5　5)　　4　6)　　4　7)　　9
　×　7　　×　4　　×　6　　×　6　　×　4　　× 10　　× 10

8)　　11　9)　　12　10)　　12　11)　　4　12)　　11　13)　　6　14)　　4
　×　7　　×　8　　×　4　　×　6　　×　5　　×　7　　×　7

15)　　9　16)　　7　17)　　3　18)　　6　19)　　7　20)　　11　21)　　6
　×　3　　×　8　　×　6　　×　3　　×　2　　× 10　　×　6

22)　　5　23)　　11　24)　　9　25)　　5　26)　　8　27)　　2　28)　　12
　× 10　　× 12　　×　7　　×　9　　×　4　　×　7　　×　9

29)　　3　30)　　8　31)　　5　32)　　8　33)　　9　34)　　5　35)　　7
　× 12　　× 10　　×　3　　× 10　　×　2　　×　8　　× 11

36)　　5　37)　　4　38)　　7　39)　　8　40)　　9　41)　　2　42)　　2
　×　7　　× 12　　×　9　　×　4　　×　5　　× 10　　×　2

43)　　11　44)　　3　45)　　2　46)　　6　47)　　11　48)　　12　49)　　9
　×　3　　×　3　　×　5　　×　7　　×　6　　×　4　　×　9

50)　　10　51)　　6　52)　　12　53)　　9　54)　　3　55)　　3　56)　　11
　×　2　　×　7　　× 10　　×　5　　×　2　　×　9　　× 12

57)　　9　58)　　8　59)　　2　60)　　9
　×　8　　×　9　　×　6　　×　3

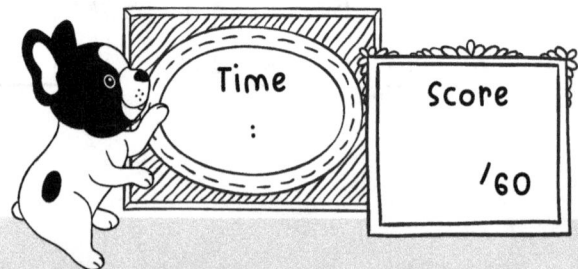

Time
:

Score

/60

DAY 94
· Mixed Questions ·

1) 5 × 8

2) 9 × 6

3) 10 × 9

4) 7 × 11

5) 7 × 10

6) 8 × 10

7) 6 × 10

8) 7 × 12

9) 6 × 3

10) 10 × 7

11) 12 × 7

12) 11 × 8

13) 10 × 9

14) 8 × 2

15) 11 × 9

16) 3 × 11

17) 8 × 9

18) 6 × 2

19) 5 × 4

20) 7 × 7

21) 2 × 10

22) 11 × 5

23) 5 × 5

24) 6 × 11

25) 7 × 12

26) 3 × 5

27) 6 × 12

28) 11 × 5

29) 3 × 3

30) 7 × 12

31) 5 × 5

32) 4 × 8

33) 6 × 7

34) 6 × 4

35) 2 × 12

36) 12 × 3

37) 12 × 10

38) 11 × 12

39) 5 × 5

40) 8 × 2

41) 10 × 10

42) 8 × 3

43) 7 × 5

44) 9 × 6

45) 11 × 11

46) 11 × 3

47) 3 × 6

48) 12 × 9

49) 6 × 8

50) 4 × 3

51) 12 × 12

52) 3 × 12

53) 8 × 7

54) 8 × 12

55) 4 × 11

56) 9 × 3

57) 7 × 4

58) 6 × 12

59) 9 × 8

60) 8 × 12

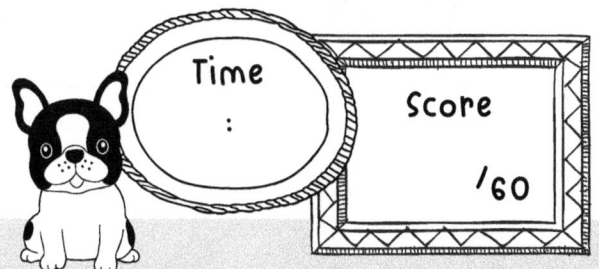

Time :

Score /60

DAY 95
· Mixed Questions ·

1) 6 × 6

2) 2 × 5

3) 12 × 12

4) 12 × 9

5) 8 × 8

6) 1 × 9

7) 8 × 9

8) 1 × 12

9) 4 × 8

10) 8 × 5

11) 4 × 9

12) 4 × 12

13) 4 × 11

14) 12 × 7

15) 4 × 5

16) 0 × 5

17) 5 × 1

18) 9 × 2

19) 6 × 9

20) 2 × 5

21) 10 × 8

22) 0 × 5

23) 6 × 6

24) 5 × 8

25) 7 × 10

26) 5 × 5

27) 6 × 4

28) 3 × 8

29) 6 × 5

30) 11 × 6

31) 5 × 12

32) 5 × 8

33) 6 × 8

34) 4 × 5

35) 4 × 7

36) 9 × 10

37) 3 × 11

38) 12 × 3

39) 4 × 12

40) 10 × 12

41) 3 × 12

42) 8 × 4

43) 6 × 2

44) 7 × 4

45) 6 × 6

46) 7 × 4

47) 3 × 7

48) 0 × 4

49) 12 × 10

50) 5 × 12

51) 12 × 1

52) 6 × 9

53) 11 × 8

54) 11 × 5

55) 2 × 4

56) 9 × 12

57) 11 × 6

58) 9 × 8

59) 4 × 6

60) 10 × 8

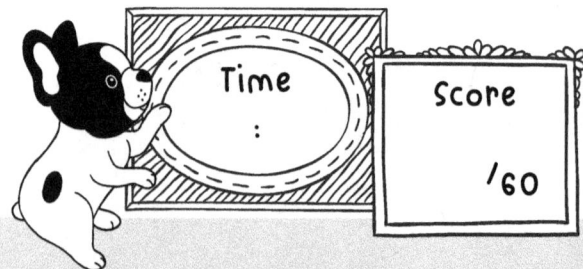

Time :

Score

/60

DAY 96
· Mixed Questions ·

1)
$$\begin{array}{r} 2 \\ \times\ 2 \\ \hline \end{array}$$

2)
$$\begin{array}{r} 6 \\ \times\ 8 \\ \hline \end{array}$$

3)
$$\begin{array}{r} 7 \\ \times\ 4 \\ \hline \end{array}$$

4)
$$\begin{array}{r} 2 \\ \times\ 7 \\ \hline \end{array}$$

5)
$$\begin{array}{r} 3 \\ \times\ 6 \\ \hline \end{array}$$

6)
$$\begin{array}{r} 11 \\ \times\ 8 \\ \hline \end{array}$$

7)
$$\begin{array}{r} 9 \\ \times\ 4 \\ \hline \end{array}$$

8)
$$\begin{array}{r} 12 \\ \times\ 6 \\ \hline \end{array}$$

9)
$$\begin{array}{r} 2 \\ \times\ 12 \\ \hline \end{array}$$

10)
$$\begin{array}{r} 8 \\ \times\ 3 \\ \hline \end{array}$$

11)
$$\begin{array}{r} 4 \\ \times\ 12 \\ \hline \end{array}$$

12)
$$\begin{array}{r} 7 \\ \times\ 10 \\ \hline \end{array}$$

13)
$$\begin{array}{r} 8 \\ \times\ 8 \\ \hline \end{array}$$

14)
$$\begin{array}{r} 6 \\ \times\ 12 \\ \hline \end{array}$$

15)
$$\begin{array}{r} 6 \\ \times\ 12 \\ \hline \end{array}$$

16)
$$\begin{array}{r} 2 \\ \times\ 12 \\ \hline \end{array}$$

17)
$$\begin{array}{r} 12 \\ \times\ 8 \\ \hline \end{array}$$

18)
$$\begin{array}{r} 4 \\ \times\ 9 \\ \hline \end{array}$$

19)
$$\begin{array}{r} 9 \\ \times\ 11 \\ \hline \end{array}$$

20)
$$\begin{array}{r} 11 \\ \times\ 9 \\ \hline \end{array}$$

21)
$$\begin{array}{r} 3 \\ \times\ 7 \\ \hline \end{array}$$

22)
$$\begin{array}{r} 9 \\ \times\ 3 \\ \hline \end{array}$$

23)
$$\begin{array}{r} 10 \\ \times\ 2 \\ \hline \end{array}$$

24)
$$\begin{array}{r} 4 \\ \times\ 8 \\ \hline \end{array}$$

25)
$$\begin{array}{r} 12 \\ \times\ 3 \\ \hline \end{array}$$

26)
$$\begin{array}{r} 11 \\ \times\ 12 \\ \hline \end{array}$$

27)
$$\begin{array}{r} 9 \\ \times\ 3 \\ \hline \end{array}$$

28)
$$\begin{array}{r} 8 \\ \times\ 8 \\ \hline \end{array}$$

29)
$$\begin{array}{r} 5 \\ \times\ 12 \\ \hline \end{array}$$

30)
$$\begin{array}{r} 7 \\ \times\ 5 \\ \hline \end{array}$$

31)
$$\begin{array}{r} 4 \\ \times\ 3 \\ \hline \end{array}$$

32)
$$\begin{array}{r} 7 \\ \times\ 7 \\ \hline \end{array}$$

33)
$$\begin{array}{r} 10 \\ \times\ 4 \\ \hline \end{array}$$

34)
$$\begin{array}{r} 2 \\ \times\ 12 \\ \hline \end{array}$$

35)
$$\begin{array}{r} 6 \\ \times\ 4 \\ \hline \end{array}$$

36)
$$\begin{array}{r} 6 \\ \times\ 11 \\ \hline \end{array}$$

37)
$$\begin{array}{r} 9 \\ \times\ 6 \\ \hline \end{array}$$

38)
$$\begin{array}{r} 4 \\ \times\ 8 \\ \hline \end{array}$$

39)
$$\begin{array}{r} 10 \\ \times\ 9 \\ \hline \end{array}$$

40)
$$\begin{array}{r} 4 \\ \times\ 2 \\ \hline \end{array}$$

41)
$$\begin{array}{r} 5 \\ \times\ 11 \\ \hline \end{array}$$

42)
$$\begin{array}{r} 12 \\ \times\ 11 \\ \hline \end{array}$$

43)
$$\begin{array}{r} 8 \\ \times\ 10 \\ \hline \end{array}$$

44)
$$\begin{array}{r} 3 \\ \times\ 11 \\ \hline \end{array}$$

45)
$$\begin{array}{r} 7 \\ \times\ 3 \\ \hline \end{array}$$

46)
$$\begin{array}{r} 2 \\ \times\ 10 \\ \hline \end{array}$$

47)
$$\begin{array}{r} 8 \\ \times\ 10 \\ \hline \end{array}$$

48)
$$\begin{array}{r} 9 \\ \times\ 8 \\ \hline \end{array}$$

49)
$$\begin{array}{r} 12 \\ \times\ 7 \\ \hline \end{array}$$

50)
$$\begin{array}{r} 8 \\ \times\ 8 \\ \hline \end{array}$$

51)
$$\begin{array}{r} 4 \\ \times\ 6 \\ \hline \end{array}$$

52)
$$\begin{array}{r} 9 \\ \times\ 3 \\ \hline \end{array}$$

53)
$$\begin{array}{r} 2 \\ \times\ 8 \\ \hline \end{array}$$

54)
$$\begin{array}{r} 11 \\ \times\ 7 \\ \hline \end{array}$$

55)
$$\begin{array}{r} 6 \\ \times\ 8 \\ \hline \end{array}$$

56)
$$\begin{array}{r} 2 \\ \times\ 5 \\ \hline \end{array}$$

57)
$$\begin{array}{r} 2 \\ \times\ 5 \\ \hline \end{array}$$

58)
$$\begin{array}{r} 6 \\ \times\ 9 \\ \hline \end{array}$$

59)
$$\begin{array}{r} 6 \\ \times\ 7 \\ \hline \end{array}$$

60)
$$\begin{array}{r} 12 \\ \times\ 11 \\ \hline \end{array}$$

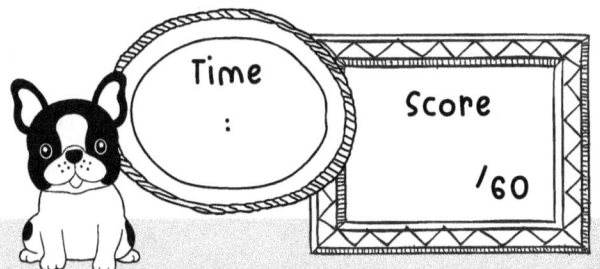

Time :

Score /60

DAY 97
· Mixed Questions ·

1) 11 × 9

2) 12 × 8

3) 5 × 6

4) 3 × 11

5) 10 × 2

6) 7 × 8

7) 3 × 5

8) 12 × 5

9) 11 × 12

10) 3 × 5

11) 8 × 3

12) 10 × 11

13) 12 × 2

14) 4 × 11

15) 3 × 5

16) 7 × 5

17) 8 × 11

18) 9 × 10

19) 12 × 8

20) 11 × 8

21) 5 × 5

22) 6 × 6

23) 7 × 3

24) 11 × 9

25) 11 × 4

26) 8 × 11

27) 3 × 10

28) 7 × 10

29) 6 × 2

30) 5 × 7

31) 3 × 4

32) 9 × 3

33) 8 × 10

34) 12 × 11

35) 8 × 12

36) 2 × 5

37) 6 × 3

38) 3 × 7

39) 4 × 5

40) 9 × 8

41) 10 × 9

42) 12 × 2

43) 4 × 4

44) 8 × 10

45) 2 × 10

46) 5 × 12

47) 2 × 7

48) 9 × 2

49) 9 × 9

50) 4 × 9

51) 6 × 8

52) 7 × 10

53) 6 × 3

54) 11 × 6

55) 3 × 10

56) 11 × 12

57) 2 × 9

58) 7 × 5

59) 11 × 5

60) 4 × 6

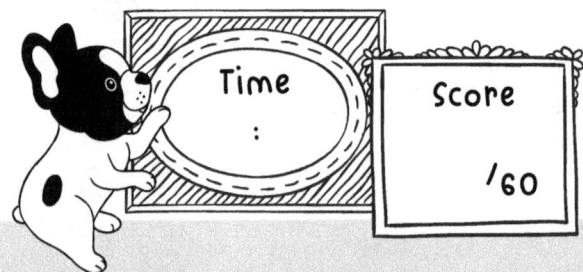

Time
:

Score

/60

DAY 98

· Mixed Questions ·

1) $\begin{array}{r} 6 \\ \times\ 7 \\ \hline \end{array}$
2) $\begin{array}{r} 6 \\ \times\ 4 \\ \hline \end{array}$
3) $\begin{array}{r} 2 \\ \times\ 9 \\ \hline \end{array}$
4) $\begin{array}{r} 6 \\ \times\ 3 \\ \hline \end{array}$
5) $\begin{array}{r} 10 \\ \times\ 8 \\ \hline \end{array}$
6) $\begin{array}{r} 4 \\ \times\ 12 \\ \hline \end{array}$
7) $\begin{array}{r} 12 \\ \times\ 12 \\ \hline \end{array}$

8) $\begin{array}{r} 4 \\ \times\ 6 \\ \hline \end{array}$
9) $\begin{array}{r} 3 \\ \times\ 7 \\ \hline \end{array}$
10) $\begin{array}{r} 2 \\ \times\ 2 \\ \hline \end{array}$
11) $\begin{array}{r} 11 \\ \times\ 4 \\ \hline \end{array}$
12) $\begin{array}{r} 10 \\ \times\ 12 \\ \hline \end{array}$
13) $\begin{array}{r} 9 \\ \times\ 5 \\ \hline \end{array}$
14) $\begin{array}{r} 7 \\ \times\ 11 \\ \hline \end{array}$

15) $\begin{array}{r} 3 \\ \times\ 9 \\ \hline \end{array}$
16) $\begin{array}{r} 2 \\ \times\ 2 \\ \hline \end{array}$
17) $\begin{array}{r} 9 \\ \times\ 3 \\ \hline \end{array}$
18) $\begin{array}{r} 5 \\ \times\ 9 \\ \hline \end{array}$
19) $\begin{array}{r} 5 \\ \times\ 4 \\ \hline \end{array}$
20) $\begin{array}{r} 10 \\ \times\ 4 \\ \hline \end{array}$
21) $\begin{array}{r} 7 \\ \times\ 9 \\ \hline \end{array}$

22) $\begin{array}{r} 7 \\ \times\ 3 \\ \hline \end{array}$
23) $\begin{array}{r} 12 \\ \times\ 6 \\ \hline \end{array}$
24) $\begin{array}{r} 9 \\ \times\ 5 \\ \hline \end{array}$
25) $\begin{array}{r} 9 \\ \times\ 8 \\ \hline \end{array}$
26) $\begin{array}{r} 4 \\ \times\ 4 \\ \hline \end{array}$
27) $\begin{array}{r} 3 \\ \times\ 11 \\ \hline \end{array}$
28) $\begin{array}{r} 8 \\ \times\ 2 \\ \hline \end{array}$

29) $\begin{array}{r} 9 \\ \times\ 6 \\ \hline \end{array}$
30) $\begin{array}{r} 3 \\ \times\ 11 \\ \hline \end{array}$
31) $\begin{array}{r} 4 \\ \times\ 7 \\ \hline \end{array}$
32) $\begin{array}{r} 7 \\ \times\ 6 \\ \hline \end{array}$
33) $\begin{array}{r} 10 \\ \times\ 11 \\ \hline \end{array}$
34) $\begin{array}{r} 10 \\ \times\ 7 \\ \hline \end{array}$
35) $\begin{array}{r} 11 \\ \times\ 8 \\ \hline \end{array}$

36) $\begin{array}{r} 12 \\ \times\ 9 \\ \hline \end{array}$
37) $\begin{array}{r} 8 \\ \times\ 10 \\ \hline \end{array}$
38) $\begin{array}{r} 7 \\ \times\ 10 \\ \hline \end{array}$
39) $\begin{array}{r} 11 \\ \times\ 12 \\ \hline \end{array}$
40) $\begin{array}{r} 11 \\ \times\ 5 \\ \hline \end{array}$
41) $\begin{array}{r} 4 \\ \times\ 5 \\ \hline \end{array}$
42) $\begin{array}{r} 12 \\ \times\ 11 \\ \hline \end{array}$

43) $\begin{array}{r} 12 \\ \times\ 12 \\ \hline \end{array}$
44) $\begin{array}{r} 6 \\ \times\ 5 \\ \hline \end{array}$
45) $\begin{array}{r} 7 \\ \times\ 2 \\ \hline \end{array}$
46) $\begin{array}{r} 3 \\ \times\ 8 \\ \hline \end{array}$
47) $\begin{array}{r} 4 \\ \times\ 5 \\ \hline \end{array}$
48) $\begin{array}{r} 6 \\ \times\ 7 \\ \hline \end{array}$
49) $\begin{array}{r} 8 \\ \times\ 7 \\ \hline \end{array}$

50) $\begin{array}{r} 6 \\ \times\ 4 \\ \hline \end{array}$
51) $\begin{array}{r} 6 \\ \times\ 6 \\ \hline \end{array}$
52) $\begin{array}{r} 2 \\ \times\ 9 \\ \hline \end{array}$
53) $\begin{array}{r} 4 \\ \times\ 2 \\ \hline \end{array}$
54) $\begin{array}{r} 8 \\ \times\ 6 \\ \hline \end{array}$
55) $\begin{array}{r} 4 \\ \times\ 6 \\ \hline \end{array}$
56) $\begin{array}{r} 6 \\ \times\ 4 \\ \hline \end{array}$

57) $\begin{array}{r} 9 \\ \times\ 5 \\ \hline \end{array}$
58) $\begin{array}{r} 10 \\ \times\ 2 \\ \hline \end{array}$
59) $\begin{array}{r} 6 \\ \times\ 8 \\ \hline \end{array}$
60) $\begin{array}{r} 10 \\ \times\ 5 \\ \hline \end{array}$

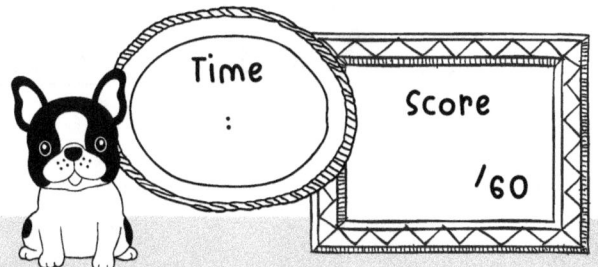

Time :

Score /60

DAY 99
· Mixed Questions ·

1) 7 × 11

2) 4 × 9

3) 9 × 4

4) 7 × 6

5) 11 × 11

6) 3 × 9

7) 5 × 4

8) 4 × 7

9) 4 × 7

10) 11 × 3

11) 3 × 11

12) 10 × 6

13) 4 × 2

14) 11 × 9

15) 9 × 10

16) 5 × 12

17) 8 × 4

18) 12 × 4

19) 7 × 12

20) 5 × 6

21) 11 × 5

22) 9 × 6

23) 10 × 12

24) 2 × 6

25) 5 × 5

26) 5 × 11

27) 7 × 2

28) 3 × 6

29) 3 × 12

30) 8 × 5

31) 8 × 2

32) 10 × 5

33) 9 × 11

34) 7 × 12

35) 12 × 2

36) 8 × 6

37) 7 × 4

38) 4 × 5

39) 8 × 10

40) 11 × 7

41) 8 × 2

42) 9 × 6

43) 11 × 6

44) 7 × 6

45) 9 × 11

46) 7 × 4

47) 7 × 4

48) 3 × 4

49) 5 × 7

50) 5 × 12

51) 4 × 3

52) 8 × 6

53) 8 × 5

54) 5 × 2

55) 9 × 3

56) 3 × 3

57) 4 × 12

58) 8 × 10

59) 11 × 12

60) 4 × 11

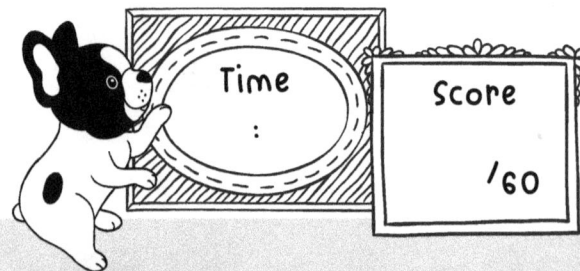

Time :

Score /60

DAY 100
· Mixed Questions ·

1) 3
× 10

2) 8
× 10

3) 10
× 8

4) 9
× 5

5) 11
× 7

6) 5
× 8

7) 10
× 6

8) 3
× 7

9) 10
× 10

10) 10
× 4

11) 9
× 8

12) 9
× 2

13) 5
× 11

14) 10
× 8

15) 9
× 7

16) 4
× 6

17) 7
× 9

18) 6
× 8

19) 10
× 7

20) 5
× 6

21) 10
× 2

22) 4
× 12

23) 4
× 3

24) 10
× 4

25) 2
× 2

26) 2
× 12

27) 2
× 10

28) 7
× 2

29) 8
× 2

30) 7
× 12

31) 12
× 9

32) 11
× 6

33) 4
× 10

34) 10
× 8

35) 7
× 7

36) 11
× 8

37) 3
× 9

38) 8
× 4

39) 9
× 6

40) 5
× 10

41) 7
× 12

42) 2
× 11

43) 12
× 5

44) 8
× 5

45) 6
× 2

46) 11
× 4

47) 5
× 12

48) 9
× 4

49) 9
× 5

50) 11
× 3

51) 12
× 2

52) 12
× 10

53) 7
× 6

54) 5
× 12

55) 6
× 8

56) 9
× 6

57) 6
× 7

58) 8
× 3

59) 10
× 5

60) 12
× 2

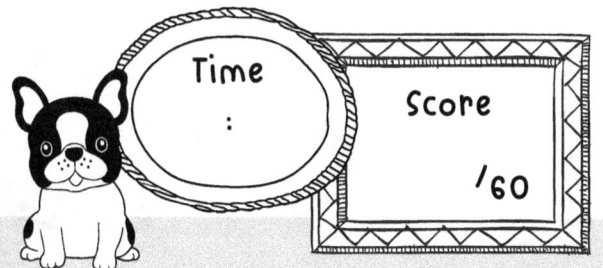

Time
:

Score

/60

FREE BONUS

Well, I hope you had a really fun and exciting time learning about multiplication, and all the cool math facts that are out there. Wait, there's more!

Join me once again and dive into the captivating stories of extraordinary sport heroes and fearless entrepreneurs. I can't wait to share their remarkable tales of innovation and determination with you. In addition to the inspiring stories, I have included some fantastic coloring pages that will spark your creativity too!

So, what are you waiting for? Claim the freebies by scanning the QR code below or type riccagarden.com/ronny_freebies into your web browser.

Your Frenchie,

RONNY

(Note: You must be 16 years or older to sign up, so grab your parent for help if you need to.)

THE
REMARKABLE
STORIES
OF DREAMERS, SPORTS STARS
AND CHILD HEROES

GET INSPIRED WITH

RONNY the FRENCHIE

The Stars

YOU WILL SHINE
AMONG THEM LIKE STARS
IN THE SKY AS YOU HOLD FIRM
THE WORD OF LIFE Philippians

IN PEACE
I WILL LIE DOWN & SLEEP,
FOR YOU ALONE O LORD,
MAKE ME DWELL IN
SAFETY.

Psalm 4:8

ANSWER KEY 🐾

DAY 1
(1)8 (2)3 (3)9 (4)8 (5)0 (6)3 (7)0 (8)1 (9)0 (10)0 (11)0 (12)2 (13)0 (14)5 (15)0 (16)0 (17)4 (18)0 (19)0 (20)2 (21)5 (22)7 (23)0 (24)9 (25)0 (26)5 (27)6 (28)1 (29)8 (30)0 (31)8 (32)6 (33)3 (34)0 (35)0 (36)0 (37)2 (38)1 (39)0 (40)0 (41)0 (42)0 (43)0 (44)1 (45)5 (46)3 (47)5 (48)3 (49)9 (50)6 (51)0 (52)1 (53)7 (54)0 (55)0 (56)0 (57)0 (58)2 (59)0 (60)4

DAY 2
(1)0 (2)7 (3)0 (4)0 (5)0 (6)0 (7)7 (8)2 (9)10 (10)0 (11)0 (12)0 (13)10 (14)9 (15)9 (16)0 (17)8 (18)7 (19)10 (20)0 (21)10 (22)0 (23)0 (24)6 (25)0 (26)1 (27)0 (28)12 (29)0 (30)1 (31)3 (32)4 (33)0 (34)0 (35)5 (36)0 (37)1 (38)9 (39)0 (40)0 (41)1 (42)2 (43)0 (44)2 (45)8 (46)0 (47)12 (48)6 (49)0 (50)3 (51)8 (52)0 (53)0 (54)0 (55)0 (56)0 (57)1 (58)0 (59)0 (60)0

DAY 3
(1)8 (2)0 (3)0 (4)3 (5)0 (6)10 (7)0 (8)0 (9)6 (10)3 (11)0 (12)11 (13)8 (14)10 (15)2 (16)12 (17)12 (18)0 (19)3 (20)12 (21)0 (22)0 (23)0 (24)0 (25)0 (26)5 (27)11 (28)5 (29)1 (30)0 (31)0 (32)0 (33)3 (34)6 (35)0 (36)0 (37)0 (38)0 (39)12 (40)0 (41)1 (42)0 (43)8 (44)0 (45)0 (46)5 (47)0 (48)0 (49)12 (50)0 (51)0 (52)0 (53)1 (54)0 (55)0 (56)9 (57)0 (58)6 (59)9 (60)2

DAY 4
(1)10 (2)12 (3)6 (4)6 (5)6 (6)12 (7)18 (8)8 (9)4 (10)12 (11)16 (12)4 (13)18 (14)10 (15)4 (16)14 (17)14 (18)12 (19)4 (20)14 (21)6 (22)8 (23)16 (24)10 (25)16 (26)12 (27)10 (28)12 (29)14 (30)14 (31)6 (32)10 (33)12 (34)4 (35)6 (36)10 (37)18 (38)18 (39)8 (40)12 (41)18 (42)12 (43)10 (44)4 (45)8 (46)8 (47)8 (48)8 (49)14 (50)10 (51)12 (52)16 (53)6 (54)18 (55)16 (56)8 (57)8 (58)4 (59)14 (60)18

DAY 5
(1)8 (2)8 (3)14 (4)12 (5)18 (6)18 (7)18 (8)4 (9)12 (10)12 (11)14 (12)8 (13)14 (14)4 (15)8 (16)18 (17)4 (18)18 (19)12 (20)12 (21)12 (22)8 (23)18 (24)8 (25)16 (26)16 (27)12 (28)4 (29)10 (30)10 (31)18 (32)18 (33)4 (34)10 (35)8 (36)12 (37)4 (38)4 (39)8 (40)10 (41)18 (42)10 (43)12 (44)18 (45)18 (46)4 (47)12 (48)10 (49)10 (50)10 (51)4 (52)4 (53)6 (54)8 (55)14 (56)6 (57)16 (58)18 (59)8 (60)12

DAY 6
(1)8 (2)10 (3)8 (4)4 (5)14 (6)18 (7)6 (8)16 (9)14 (10)2 (11)14 (12)10 (13)18 (14)14 (15)18 (16)12 (17)18 (18)10 (19)6 (20)10 (21)10 (22)16 (23)6 (24)10 (25)6 (26)10 (27)10 (28)8 (29)8 (30)4 (31)10 (32)8 (33)12 (34)14 (35)4 (36)0 (37)0 (38)12 (39)10 (40)16 (41)16 (42)4 (43)2 (44)4 (45)14 (46)12 (47)0 (48)18 (49)10 (50)8 (51)4 (52)18 (53)8 (54)18 (55)2 (56)8 (57)10 (58)6 (59)14 (60)6

DAY 7
(1)10 (2)12 (3)4 (4)16 (5)4 (6)14 (7)10 (8)10 (9)14 (10)6 (11)10 (12)16 (13)18 (14)14 (15)10 (16)8 (17)6 (18)16 (19)8 (20)10 (21)6 (22)8 (23)18 (24)18 (25)10 (26)8 (27)6 (28)14 (29)16 (30)6 (31)4 (32)16 (33)4 (34)6 (35)6 (36)12 (37)14 (38)6 (39)18 (40)18 (41)16 (42)14 (43)4 (44)14 (45)14 (46)6 (47)18 (48)6 (49)18 (50)14 (51)10 (52)4 (53)18 (54)14 (55)8 (56)16 (57)8 (58)18 (59)12 (60)6

DAY 8
(1)12 (2)20 (3)12 (4)6 (5)6 (6)4 (7)24 (8)24 (9)22 (10)6 (11)8 (12)14 (13)6 (14)16 (15)14 (16)14 (17)10 (18)20 (19)22 (20)20 (21)20 (22)20 (23)12 (24)8 (25)22 (26)18 (27)18 (28)6 (29)4 (30)12 (31)8 (32)10 (33)12 (34)4 (35)10 (36)16 (37)14 (38)16 (39)16 (40)10 (41)14 (42)4 (43)4 (44)10 (45)16 (46)10 (47)24 (48)22 (49)18 (50)8 (51)16 (52)12 (53)16 (54)14 (55)6 (56)6 (57)20 (58)18 (59)24 (60)12

DAY 9
(1)0 (2)22 (3)12 (4)12 (5)14 (6)22 (7)4 (8)18 (9)6 (10)24 (11)12 (12)8 (13)4 (14)16 (15)4 (16)24 (17)6 (18)22 (19)6 (20)14 (21)10 (22)4 (23)14 (24)10 (25)16 (26)6 (27)4 (28)8 (29)22 (30)0 (31)18 (32)20 (33)14 (34)4 (35)24 (36)2 (37)12 (38)8 (39)18 (40)2 (41)2 (42)14 (43)18 (44)10 (45)0 (46)10 (47)16 (48)16 (49)2 (50)14 (51)8 (52)8 (53)18 (54)18 (55)8 (56)8 (57)2 (58)14 (59)14 (60)24

DAY 10
(1)22 (2)12 (3)8 (4)20 (5)20 (6)20 (7)14 (8)8 (9)16 (10)22 (11)6 (12)8 (13)24 (14)24 (15)12 (16)24 (17)6 (18)6 (19)12 (20)14 (21)22 (22)22 (23)14 (24)14 (25)4 (26)24 (27)24 (28)4 (29)20 (30)24 (31)4 (32)22 (33)10 (34)8 (35)18 (36)24 (37)14 (38)20 (39)24 (40)14 (41)20 (42)12 (43)18 (44)12 (45)22 (46)6 (47)16 (48)12 (49)18 (50)22 (51)20 (52)24 (53)8 (54)14 (55)16 (56)12 (57)20 (58)18 (59)24 (60)20

DAY 11
(1)14 (2)24 (3)12 (4)4 (5)20 (6)16 (7)14 (8)14 (9)12 (10)10 (11)20 (12)10 (13)10 (14)4 (15)4 (16)6 (17)6 (18)20 (19)18 (20)16 (21)8 (22)20 (23)12 (24)14 (25)4 (26)22 (27)24 (28)16 (29)8 (30)24 (31)10 (32)4 (33)14 (34)18 (35)18 (36)22 (37)10 (38)14 (39)4 (40)4 (41)6 (42)14 (43)4 (44)16 (45)10 (46)8 (47)14 (48)18 (49)10 (50)16 (51)8 (52)12 (53)16 (54)4 (55)10 (56)18 (57)14 (58)8 (59)12 (60)20

DAY 12
(1)24 (2)21 (3)18 (4)15 (5)15 (6)27 (7)21 (8)15 (9)18 (10)18 (11)27 (12)24 (13)12 (14)15 (15)6 (16)15 (17)6 (18)18 (19)24 (20)24 (21)12 (22)21 (23)12 (24)27 (25)21 (26)15 (27)24 (28)12 (29)21 (30)9 (31)27 (32)15 (33)12 (34)12 (35)9 (36)27 (37)21 (38)18 (39)15 (40)21 (41)27 (42)21 (43)6 (44)24 (45)27 (46)21 (47)15 (48)12 (49)12 (50)21 (51)12 (52)6 (53)6 (54)24 (55)12 (56)27 (57)27 (58)27 (59)9 (60)27

DAY 13
(1)24 (2)15 (3)21 (4)15 (5)9 (6)24 (7)12 (8)12 (9)24 (10)15 (11)21 (12)6 (13)27 (14)21 (15)21 (16)24 (17)18 (18)18 (19)12 (20)15 (21)6 (22)27 (23)18 (24)27 (25)6 (26)12 (27)21 (28)18 (29)21 (30)18 (31)15 (32)9 (33)12 (34)12 (35)9 (36)27 (37)15 (38)6 (39)24 (40)27 (41)18 (42)24 (43)15 (44)18 (45)27 (46)18 (47)18 (48)6 (49)12 (50)15 (51)12 (52)15 (53)18 (54)12 (55)15 (56)18 (57)6 (58)6 (59)24 (60)12

DAY 14
(1)27 (2)21 (3)24 (4)3 (5)6 (6)12 (7)6 (8)0 (9)15 (10)12 (11)18 (12)0 (13)9 (14)24 (15)18 (16)12 (17)27 (18)24 (19)18 (20)6 (21)18 (22)12 (23)24 (24)0 (25)12 (26)21 (27)6 (28)6 (29)24 (30)21 (31)21 (32)12 (33)3 (34)18 (35)21 (36)3 (37)6 (38)9 (39)15 (40)18 (41)18 (42)24 (43)27 (44)18 (45)24 (46)18 (47)9 (48)0 (49)3 (50)3 (51)6 (52)3 (53)24 (54)6 (55)27 (56)24 (57)21 (58)3 (59)24 (60)12

DAY 15
(1)21 (2)27 (3)21 (4)27 (5)15 (6)12 (7)9 (8)6 (9)21 (10)21 (11)21 (12)18 (13)21 (14)12 (15)12 (16)21 (17)15 (18)21 (19)6 (20)12 (21)9 (22)24 (23)18 (24)6 (25)24 (26)27 (27)18 (28)27 (29)27 (30)6 (31)24 (32)6 (33)27 (34)6 (35)15 (36)18 (37)18 (38)18 (39)27 (40)18 (41)6 (42)21 (43)21 (44)9 (45)9 (46)24 (47)12 (48)21 (49)9 (50)24 (51)24 (52)24 (53)24 (54)27 (55)27 (56)6 (57)18 (58)27 (59)15 (60)12

ANSWER KEY 🐾

DAY 16
(1)36 (2)15 (3)3 (4)6 (5)21 (6)12 (7)9 (8)18
(9)12 (10)36 (11)33 (12)12 (13)30 (14)18
(15)0 (16)9 (17)18 (18)27 (19)27 (20)18
(21)24 (22)36 (23)18 (24)21 (25)18 (26)12
(27)24 (28)24 (29)21 (30)15 (31)15 (32)12
(33)18 (34)33 (35)36 (36)27 (37)36 (38)18
(39)9 (40)6 (41)21 (42)3 (43)0 (44)3
(45)18 (46)27 (47)18 (48)30 (49)15 (50)30
(51)18 (52)9 (53)9 (54)9 (55)3 (56)12
(57)3 (58)6 (59)27 (60)6

DAY 17
(1)27 (2)9 (3)36 (4)33 (5)30 (6)30 (7)9
(8)30 (9)33 (10)21 (11)24 (12)30 (13)15
(14)21 (15)15 (16)33 (17)21 (18)9 (19)27
(20)6 (21)30 (22)27 (23)18 (24)33 (25)12
(26)18 (27)30 (28)24 (29)6 (30)30 (31)18
(32)36 (33)30 (34)27 (35)21 (36)33 (37)24
(38)15 (39)21 (40)30 (41)12 (42)24 (43)15
(44)18 (45)27 (46)6 (47)30 (48)27 (49)21
(50)24 (51)30 (52)24 (53)24 (54)27 (55)9
(56)24 (57)24 (58)9 (59)12 (60)15

DAY 18
(1)6 (2)36 (3)33 (4)15 (5)36 (6)33 (7)33
(8)12 (9)18 (10)6 (11)36 (12)27 (13)15
(14)21 (15)21 (16)21 (17)33 (18)12 (19)18
(20)12 (21)12 (22)12 (23)12 (24)30 (25)24
(26)6 (27)30 (28)9 (29)24 (30)30 (31)9
(32)18 (33)21 (34)15 (35)18 (36)27 (37)12
(38)24 (39)30 (40)15 (41)27 (42)24 (43)15
(44)30 (45)15 (46)27 (47)36 (48)15 (49)6
(50)21 (51)18 (52)18 (53)27 (54)21 (55)33
(56)18 (57)6 (58)24 (59)12 (60)21

DAY 19
(1)18 (2)24 (3)6 (4)24 (5)9 (6)6 (7)12 (8)30
(9)6 (10)12 (11)30 (12)15 (13)9 (14)27
(15)15 (16)30 (17)24 (18)15 (19)15 (20)30
(21)15 (22)12 (23)30 (24)30 (25)33 (26)36
(27)33 (28)27 (29)33 (30)27 (31)30 (32)9
(33)9 (34)36 (35)18 (36)18 (37)6 (38)9
(39)30 (40)27 (41)24 (42)30 (43)12 (44)21
(45)6 (46)12 (47)21 (48)21 (49)6 (50)18
(51)18 (52)18 (53)24 (54)36 (55)33 (56)15
(57)27 (58)15 (59)36 (60)36

DAY 20
(1)12 (2)0 (3)20 (4)20 (5)24 (6)32 (7)16
(8)36 (9)4 (10)20 (11)16 (12)0 (13)8
(14)12 (15)32 (16)32 (17)8 (18)20 (19)32
(20)12 (21)28 (22)36 (23)0 (24)12 (25)8
(26)20 (27)8 (28)20 (29)0 (30)28 (31)12
(32)0 (33)8 (34)28 (35)32 (36)24 (37)28
(38)12 (39)4 (40)24 (41)16 (42)8 (43)24
(44)28 (45)20 (46)20 (47)32 (48)8 (49)28
(50)16 (51)36 (52)4 (53)24 (54)36 (55)0
(56)28 (57)12 (58)36 (59)24 (60)20

DAY 21
(1)32 (2)36 (3)12 (4)24 (5)20 (6)16 (7)12
(8)12 (9)20 (10)36 (11)28 (12)28 (13)8
(14)28 (15)36 (16)16 (17)36 (18)12 (19)24
(20)16 (21)20 (22)32 (23)32 (24)8 (25)24
(26)8 (27)12 (28)24 (29)8 (30)32 (31)36
(32)24 (33)16 (34)12 (35)32 (36)8 (37)36
(38)32 (39)32 (40)28 (41)32 (42)20 (43)36
(44)16 (45)28 (46)32 (47)28 (48)8 (49)24
(50)16 (51)36 (52)20 (53)20 (54)28 (55)12
(56)36 (57)12 (58)32 (59)28 (60)12

DAY 22
(1)28 (2)24 (3)8 (4)24 (5)28 (6)28 (7)36
(8)16 (9)28 (10)16 (11)36 (12)8 (13)12
(14)20 (15)8 (16)36 (17)28 (18)20 (19)28
(20)12 (21)24 (22)20 (23)32 (24)8 (25)24
(26)8 (27)36 (28)24 (29)32 (30)32 (31)20
(32)20 (33)36 (34)16 (35)12 (36)36 (37)32
(38)12 (39)28 (40)36 (41)24 (42)20 (43)8
(44)24 (45)12 (46)24 (47)32 (48)32 (49)36
(50)24 (51)32 (52)8 (53)32 (54)20 (55)24
(56)12 (57)28 (58)12 (59)8 (60)28

DAY 23
(1)36 (2)16 (3)36 (4)20 (5)36 (6)36 (7)36
(8)8 (9)36 (10)32 (11)20 (12)32 (13)36
(14)16 (15)8 (16)24 (17)28 (18)16 (19)28
(20)28 (21)16 (22)36 (23)20 (24)36 (25)8
(26)28 (27)24 (28)8 (29)28 (30)8 (31)20
(32)36 (33)36 (34)36 (35)36 (36)24 (37)16
(38)32 (39)20 (40)20 (41)24 (42)32 (43)24
(44)36 (45)36 (46)20 (47)8 (48)8 (49)24
(50)24 (51)20 (52)36 (53)16 (54)28 (55)8
(56)32 (57)32 (58)8 (59)8 (60)32

DAY 24
(1)12 (2)36 (3)44 (4)44 (5)40 (6)24 (7)20
(8)12 (9)36 (10)32 (11)24 (12)44 (13)12
(14)48 (15)12 (16)48 (17)16 (18)24 (19)44
(20)28 (21)12 (22)24 (23)20 (24)32 (25)44
(26)28 (27)32 (28)16 (29)48 (30)20 (31)28
(32)36 (33)20 (34)12 (35)36 (36)28 (37)12
(38)28 (39)20 (40)24 (41)32 (42)20 (43)32
(44)28 (45)8 (46)8 (47)16 (48)40 (49)44
(50)16 (51)48 (52)32 (53)36 (54)32 (55)44
(56)28 (57)40 (58)12 (59)48 (60)16

DAY 25
(1)44 (2)32 (3)16 (4)48 (5)16 (6)48 (7)20
(8)4 (9)4 (10)0 (11)12 (12)24 (13)28
(14)48 (15)36 (16)8 (17)28 (18)48 (19)36
(20)20 (21)8 (22)4 (23)32 (24)32 (25)4
(26)24 (27)0 (28)36 (29)48 (30)20 (31)24
(32)36 (33)28 (34)24 (35)8 (36)4 (37)20
(38)44 (39)24 (40)28 (41)44 (42)40 (43)32
(44)16 (45)36 (46)24 (47)44 (48)48 (49)36
(50)36 (51)32 (52)28 (53)12 (54)16 (55)16
(56)44 (57)8 (58)12 (59)16 (60)12

DAY 26
(1)20 (2)44 (3)44 (4)24 (5)20 (6)24 (7)40
(8)44 (9)40 (10)16 (11)12 (12)36 (13)40
(14)32 (15)20 (16)16 (17)8 (18)24 (19)20
(20)24 (21)28 (22)28 (23)36 (24)8 (25)12
(26)16 (27)12 (28)44 (29)28 (30)12 (31)8
(32)36 (33)20 (34)44 (35)44 (36)24 (37)28
(38)8 (39)8 (40)32 (41)8 (42)24 (43)8
(44)12 (45)48 (46)40 (47)36 (48)32 (49)24
(50)16 (51)36 (52)8 (53)32 (54)12 (55)12
(56)28 (57)20 (58)12 (59)44 (60)44

DAY 27
(1)36 (2)16 (3)24 (4)24 (5)8 (6)24 (7)32
(8)24 (9)36 (10)12 (11)20 (12)28 (13)32
(14)36 (15)12 (16)16 (17)32 (18)20 (19)12
(20)36 (21)32 (22)48 (23)36 (24)32 (25)28
(26)12 (27)40 (28)48 (29)40 (30)16 (31)48
(32)44 (33)36 (34)36 (35)8 (36)36 (37)40
(38)44 (39)24 (40)16 (41)48 (42)20 (43)24
(44)32 (45)24 (46)28 (47)8 (48)24 (49)12
(50)12 (51)28 (52)16 (53)36 (54)44 (55)24
(56)44 (57)20 (58)28 (59)24 (60)44

DAY 28
(1)45 (2)25 (3)45 (4)30 (5)45 (6)20 (7)35
(8)25 (9)35 (10)35 (11)25 (12)25 (13)20
(14)20 (15)10 (16)25 (17)35 (18)30 (19)20
(20)40 (21)20 (22)30 (23)15 (24)25 (25)30
(26)25 (27)20 (28)25 (29)10 (30)30 (31)20
(32)10 (33)45 (34)25 (35)20 (36)25 (37)40
(38)45 (39)20 (40)40 (41)25 (42)25 (43)15
(44)30 (45)35 (46)10 (47)30 (48)25 (49)45
(50)45 (51)45 (52)35 (53)45 (54)15 (55)45
(56)15 (57)40 (58)15 (59)45 (60)40

DAY 29
(1)20 (2)45 (3)40 (4)15 (5)30 (6)20 (7)40
(8)40 (9)15 (10)40 (11)30 (12)20 (13)30
(14)25 (15)10 (16)25 (17)15 (18)25 (19)15
(20)40 (21)45 (22)40 (23)40 (24)30 (25)15
(26)40 (27)35 (28)35 (29)35 (30)45 (31)35
(32)10 (33)45 (34)20 (35)30 (36)25 (37)25
(38)20 (39)25 (40)45 (41)45 (42)30 (43)25
(44)30 (45)15 (46)35 (47)45 (48)15 (49)30
(50)10 (51)35 (52)15 (53)25 (54)40 (55)30
(56)20 (57)25 (58)20 (59)40 (60)10

DAY 30
(1)40 (2)25 (3)10 (4)0 (5)15 (6)25 (7)15
(8)10 (9)40 (10)40 (11)25 (12)40 (13)5
(14)40 (15)40 (16)15 (17)35 (18)25 (19)45
(20)35 (21)5 (22)15 (23)35 (24)25 (25)15
(26)40 (27)35 (28)10 (29)0 (30)5 (31)35
(32)30 (33)30 (34)35 (35)40 (36)15 (37)20
(38)25 (39)30 (40)30 (41)15 (42)45 (43)20
(44)10 (45)35 (46)40 (47)30 (48)25 (49)40
(50)15 (51)5 (52)0 (53)10 (54)35 (55)0
(56)30 (57)0 (58)20 (59)45 (60)20

ANSWER KEY 🐾

DAY 31
(1)20 (2)25 (3)45 (4)10 (5)20 (6)40 (7)3 0
(8)25 (9)45 (10)25 (11)25 (12)10 (13)20
(14)15 (15)30 (16)45 (17)15 (18)10 (19)10
(20)40 (21)25 (22)20 (23)30 (24)30 (25)20
(26)25 (27)10 (28)35 (29)30 (30)20 (31)15
(32)40 (33)35 (34)35 (35)25 (36)35 (37)45
(38)20 (39)15 (40)40 (41)10 (42)10 (43)40
(44)35 (45)30 (46)10 (47)35 (48)35 (49)40
(50)25 (51)10 (52)15 (53)10 (54)40 (55)35
(56)25 (57)25 (58)45 (59)15 (60)15

DAY 32
(1)40 (2)60 (3)20 (4)50 (5)35 (6)45 (7)5 5
(8)10 (9)20 (10)30 (11)50 (12)40 (13)55
(14)45 (15)10 (16)10 (17)60 (18)10 (19)25
(20)25 (21)20 (22)40 (23)20 (24)60 (25)40
(26)30 (27)55 (28)25 (29)45 (30)35 (31)20
(32)30 (33)30 (34)20 (35)45 (36)10 (37)10
(38)45 (39)60 (40)40 (41)30 (42)50 (43)35
(44)35 (45)15 (46)15 (47)30 (48)20 (49)60
(50)45 (51)30 (52)30 (53)25 (54)50 (55)5 0
(56)55 (57)15 (58)10 (59)15 (60)25

DAY 33
(1)35 (2)30 (3)45 (4)0 (5)20 (6)50 (7) 0
(8)15 (9)10 (10)35 (11)50 (12)5 (13)55
(14)20 (15)10 (16)35 (17)30 (18)0 (19)5 5
(20)60 (21)5 (22)0 (23)55 (24)5 (25)55
(26)0 (27)55 (28)45 (29)40 (30)25 (31) 0
(32)50 (33)15 (34)55 (35)60 (36)20 (37)15
(38)60 (39)15 (40)15 (41)45 (42)25 (43) 0
(44)50 (45)35 (46)55 (47)10 (48)60 (49)35
(50)45 (51)40 (52)10 (53)45 (54)30 (55)35
(56)50 (57)25 (58)25 (59)15 (60)15

DAY 34
(1)35 (2)40 (3)15 (4)40 (5)20 (6)20 (7)2 5
(8)30 (9)20 (10)55 (11)35 (12)45 (13)1 0
(14)45 (15)25 (16)60 (17)60 (18)10 (19)30
(20)10 (21)10 (22)10 (23)25 (24)20 (25)15
(26)15 (27)10 (28)40 (29)25 (30)55 (31)45
(32)30 (33)10 (34)50 (35)55 (36)15 (37)45
(38)10 (39)25 (40)40 (41)60 (42)45 (43)20
(44)30 (45)20 (46)25 (47)45 (48)55 (49)20
(50)50 (51)35 (52)40 (53)30 (54)25 (55)15
(56)10 (57)50 (58)25 (59)55 (60)60

DAY 35
(1)20 (2)35 (3)20 (4)45 (5)60 (6)10 (7)15
(8)10 (9)60 (10)25 (11)60 (12)55 (13)20
(14)50 (15)10 (16)40 (17)35 (18)40 (19)15
(20)50 (21)30 (22)35 (23)20 (24)20 (25)20
(26)55 (27)40 (28)20 (29)45 (30)15 (31)25
(32)25 (33)25 (34)15 (35)20 (36)60 (37)60
(38)50 (39)50 (40)20 (41)55 (42)50 (43)55
(44)25 (45)60 (46)40 (47)25 (48)10 (49)15
(50)35 (51)55 (52)10 (53)10 (54)10 (55)55
(56)30 (57)25 (58)50 (59)30 (60)55

DAY 36
(1)48 (2)18 (3)36 (4)30 (5)36 (6)42 (7)5 4
(8)36 (9)12 (10)30 (11)24 (12)24 (13)36
(14)42 (15)30 (16)30 (17)54 (18)24 (19)48
(20)30 (21)42 (22)36 (23)54 (24)18 (25)48
(26)36 (27)36 (28)12 (29)24 (30)36 (31)54
(32)42 (33)18 (34)30 (35)42 (36)48 (37)42
(38)36 (39)36 (40)30 (41)36 (42)12 (43)54
(44)42 (45)48 (46)24 (47)30 (48)24 (49)36
(50)18 (51)48 (52)24 (53)12 (54)36 (55)30
(56)12 (57)30 (58)12 (59)36 (60)12

DAY 37
(1)0 (2)30 (3)0 (4)18 (5)18 (6)36 (7)6 (8)36
(9)48 (10)6 (11)42 (12)0 (13)54 (14)30
(15)12 (16)48 (17)12 (18)42 (19)54 (20)36
(21)36 (22)42 (23)18 (24)36 (25)48 (26)54
(27)24 (28)30 (29)54 (30)30 (31)6 (32)48
(33)6 (34)18 (35)6 (36)24 (37)36 (38)12
(39)42 (40)36 (41)42 (42)36 (43)36 (44)18
(45)0 (46)12 (47)30 (48)30 (49)6 (50)5 4
(51)24 (52)0 (53)30 (54)42 (55)6 (56)1 8
(57)6 (58)48 (59)0 (60)42

DAY 38
(1)54 (2)36 (3)18 (4)30 (5)30 (6)24 (7)3 0
(8)12 (9)48 (10)12 (11)18 (12)12 (13)12
(14)30 (15)30 (16)42 (17)36 (18)42 (19)12
(20)30 (21)18 (22)30 (23)36 (24)24 (25)42
(26)30 (27)12 (28)24 (29)12 (30)18 (31)48
(32)24 (33)36 (34)48 (35)30 (36)18 (37)36
(38)24 (39)12 (40)42 (41)24 (42)36 (43)54
(44)18 (45)54 (46)42 (47)54 (48)42 (49)12
(50)24 (51)54 (52)54 (53)18 (54)12 (55)54
(56)18 (57)42 (58)48 (59)24 (60)30

DAY 39
(1)36 (2)12 (3)48 (4)42 (5)54 (6)30 (7)5 4
(8)36 (9)18 (10)30 (11)36 (12)54 (13)5 4
(14)54 (15)48 (16)42 (17)48 (18)42 (19)24
(20)12 (21)48 (22)36 (23)48 (24)48 (25)48
(26)12 (27)54 (28)30 (29)36 (30)48 (31)18
(32)18 (33)54 (34)30 (35)36 (36)12 (37)42
(38)24 (39)24 (40)36 (41)36 (42)54 (43)48
(44)48 (45)24 (46)18 (47)18 (48)18 (49)24
(50)12 (51)54 (52)48 (53)54 (54)54 (55)12
(56)42 (57)30 (58)48 (59)18 (60)12

DAY 40
(1)18 (2)12 (3)66 (4)12 (5)72 (6)54 (7)42
(8)54 (9)54 (10)48 (11)60 (12)42 (13)48
(14)24 (15)30 (16)66 (17)30 (18)30 (19)72
(20)54 (21)42 (22)48 (23)42 (24)30 (25)18
(26)30 (27)18 (28)36 (29)12 (30)66 (31)18
(32)42 (33)48 (34)12 (35)66 (36)30 (37)42
(38)54 (39)18 (40)66 (41)48 (42)12 (43)60
(44)36 (45)36 (46)24 (47)24 (48)30 (49)30
(50)60 (51)42 (52)66 (53)18 (54)24 (55)48
(56)24 (57)24 (58)54 (59)42 (60)18

DAY 41
(1)30 (2)24 (3)36 (4)24 (5)72 (6)66 (7)3 6
(8)48 (9)66 (10)24 (11)48 (12)66 (13)48
(14)42 (15)42 (16)30 (17)18 (18)66 (19)36
(20)24 (21)48 (22)48 (23)30 (24)60 (25)12
(26)54 (27)72 (28)24 (29)18 (30)18 (31)54
(32)36 (33)66 (34)48 (35)24 (36)36 (37)54
(38)72 (39)54 (40)66 (41)66 (42)30 (43)72
(44)72 (45)30 (46)48 (47)36 (48)66 (49)36
(50)18 (51)42 (52)18 (53)36 (54)18 (55)60
(56)30 (57)30 (58)36 (59)24 (60)72

DAY 42
(1)0 (2)24 (3)6 (4)42 (5)30 (6)0 (7)6 (8)30
(9)72 (10)18 (11)36 (12)72 (13)6 (14)12
(15)6 (16)66 (17)48 (18)30 (19)12 (20)0
(21)72 (22)54 (23)18 (24)72 (25)24 (26)18
(27)0 (28)24 (29)6 (30)48 (31)12 (32)0
(33)0 (34)48 (35)6 (36)60 (37)6 (38)36
(39)6 (40)54 (41)30 (42)66 (43)18 (44)18
(45)18 (46)66 (47)72 (48)30 (49)18 (50)36
(51)72 (52)18 (53)12 (54)36 (55)42 (56)54
(57)6 (58)36 (59)48 (60)60

DAY 43
(1)30 (2)60 (3)54 (4)18 (5)72 (6)30 (7)1 2
(8)60 (9)72 (10)72 (11)36 (12)54 (13)48
(14)42 (15)72 (16)48 (17)72 (18)18 (19) 54
(20)24 (21)24 (22)54 (23)30 (24)12 (25) 12
(26)12 (27)60 (28)30 (29)30 (30)36 (31) 12
(32)36 (33)54 (34)60 (35)12 (36)48 (37) 36
(38)66 (39)24 (40)60 (41)54 (42)66 (43) 18
(44)60 (45)18 (46)24 (47)72 (48)12 (49) 30
(50)24 (51)66 (52)12 (53)66 (54)12 (55) 30
(56)66 (57)30 (58)48 (59)42 (60)36

DAY 44
(1)56 (2)63 (3)21 (4)21 (5)42 (6)63 (7)5 6
(8)21 (9)42 (10) 0 (11)49 (12)14 (13)5 6
(14)28 (15)21 (16)21 (17)56 (18)21 (19)42
(20)49 (21)56 (22)28 (23)14 (24)56 (25)14
(26)42 (27)49 (28)42 (29)14 (30)49 (31) 0
(32)63 (33)49 (34)56 (35)14 (36)35 (37)28
(38)63 (39)14 (40)28 (41)21 (42)63 (43)28
(44)14 (45)28 (46)21 (47)35 (48)21 (49)14
(50)14 (51)63 (52)21 (53)7 (54)56 (55)56
(56)49 (57)14 (58)49 (59)42 (60)35

DAY 45
(1)56 (2)28 (3)63 (4)49 (5)42 (6)63 (7)3 5
(8)63 (9)21 (10)63 (11)56 (12)21 (13)4 2
(14)14 (15)49 (16)42 (17)21 (18)28 (19)56
(20)56 (21)14 (22)35 (23)49 (24)21 (25)63
(26)42 (27)49 (28)28 (29)42 (30)28 (31)42
(32)56 (33)21 (34)49 (35)56 (36)63 (37)21
(38)14 (39)28 (40)42 (41)14 (42)14 (43)42
(44)14 (45)35 (46)63 (47)63 (48)21 (49)21
(50)28 (51)21 (52)42 (53)42 (54)56 (55)56
(56)56 (57)56 (58)49 (59)28 (60)49

ANSWER KEY 🐾

DAY 46
(1)63 (2)49 (3)21 (4)21 (5)42 (6)21 (7)2 1
(8)28 (9)0 (10)0 (11)14 (12)42 (13)5 6
(14)28 (15)28 (16)0 (17)35 (18)35 (19)0
(20)28 (21)28 (22)35 (23)14 (24)49 (25)7
(26)7 (27)21 (28)7 (29)14 (30)42 (31)14
(32)63 (33)0 (34)63 (35)35 (36)56 (37)63
(38)49 (39)28 (40)0 (41)21 (42)35 (43)28
(44)21 (45)28 (46)49 (47)0 (48)42 (49)35
(50)14 (51)21 (52)35 (53)42 (54)63 (55)35
(56)42 (57)14 (58)56 (59)56 (60)21

DAY 47
(1)21 (2)21 (3)28 (4)21 (5)42 (6)42 (7)4 9
(8)63 (9)21 (10)28 (11)63 (12)35 (13)56
(14)56 (15)63 (16)35 (17)49 (18)35 (19)21
(20)35 (21)49 (22)14 (23)35 (24)56 (25)21
(26)14 (27)49 (28)21 (29)56 (30)49 (31)56
(32)28 (33)63 (34)63 (35)28 (36)42 (37)21
(38)56 (39)28 (40)14 (41)49 (42)35 (43)21
(44)49 (45)63 (46)28 (47)42 (48)28 (49)35
(50)35 (51)63 (52)28 (53)63 (54)56 (55)42
(56)63 (57)14 (58)28 (59)28 (60)56

DAY 48
(1)42 (2)70 (3)21 (4)14 (5)70 (6)56 (7)5 6
(8)56 (9)77 (10)77 (11)21 (12)56 (13)77
(14)42 (15)63 (16)14 (17)21 (18)70 (19)21
(20)21 (21)28 (22)14 (23)56 (24)21 (25)42
(26)70 (27)35 (28)35 (29)28 (30)56 (31)63
(32)56 (33)49 (34)77 (35)42 (36)70 (37)49
(38)70 (39)56 (40)14 (41)84 (42)56 (43)14
(44)84 (45)70 (46)56 (47)63 (48)63 (49)28
(50)49 (51)49 (52)63 (53)56 (54)35 (55)56
(56)42 (57)56 (58)56 (59)42 (60)8 4

DAY 49
(1)28 (2)63 (3)56 (4)56 (5)42 (6)14 (7)5 6
(8)84 (9)49 (10)21 (11)70 (12)70 (13)21
(14)63 (15)70 (16)14 (17)49 (18)56 (19)77
(20)84 (21)77 (22)49 (23)84 (24)84 (25)21
(26)42 (27)70 (28)35 (29)77 (30)56 (31)49
(32)63 (33)21 (34)70 (35)14 (36)21 (37)56
(38)63 (39)21 (40)42 (41)42 (42)21 (43)14
(44)84 (45)84 (46)84 (47)21 (48)56 (49)42
(50)63 (51)70 (52)14 (53)70 (54)49 (55)84
(56)21 (57)49 (58)56 (59)84 (60)77

DAY 50
(1)14 (2)28 (3)56 (4)42 (5)63 (6)7 (7)84
(8)63 (9)21 (10)42 (11)35 (12)77 (13)4 2
(14)28 (15)56 (16)14 (17)0 (18)63 (19)28
(20)84 (21)49 (22)63 (23)63 (24)70 (25)14
(26)63 (27)84 (28)21 (29)63 (30)77 (31)84
(32)49 (33)42 (34)28 (35)7 (36)7 (37)4 2
(38)56 (39)21 (40)35 (41)0 (42)7 (43)5 6
(44)21 (45)70 (46)49 (47)0 (48)77 (49)14
(50)28 (51)49 (52)35 (53)77 (54)84 (55)84
(56)77 (57)14 (58)49 (59)84 (60) 0

DAY 51
(1)84 (2)14 (3)49 (4)0 (5)42 (6)28 (7)4 2
(8)28 (9)63 (10)14 (11)28 (12)56 (13)3 5
(14)77 (15)77 (16)35 (17)84 (18)70 (19)5 6
(20)63 (21)42 (22)63 (23)56 (24)49 (25)4 2
(26)56 (27)70 (28)84 (29)56 (30)70 (31)3 5
(32)84 (33)70 (34)63 (35)70 (36)56 (37)7 7
(38)84 (39)77 (40)35 (41)63 (42)70 (43)2 8
(44)77 (45)42 (46)49 (47)63 (48)84 (49)4 9
(50)42 (51)56 (52)56 (53)56 (54)56 (55)4 2
(56)28 (57)77 (58)42 (59)63 (60)14

DAY 52
(1)48 (2)56 (3)40 (4)56 (5)32 (6)24 (7)5 6
(8)40 (9)56 (10)32 (11)48 (12)16 (13)48
(14)72 (15)24 (16)72 (17)16 (18)24 (19)16
(20)72 (21)56 (22)72 (23)72 (24)16 (25)32
(26)40 (27)40 (28)72 (29)24 (30)56 (31)48
(32)64 (33)40 (34)48 (35)56 (36)72 (37)72
(38)56 (39)40 (40)32 (41)24 (42)32 (43)32
(44)32 (45)64 (46)48 (47)72 (48)24 (49)32
(50)72 (51)32 (52)32 (53)64 (54)64 (55)48
(56)32 (57)72 (58)32 (59)16 (60)32

DAY 53
(1)56 (2)56 (3)8 (4)56 (5)64 (6)72 (7)5 6
(8)32 (9)24 (10)40 (11)8 (12)8 (13)64
(14)8 (15)32 (16)16 (17)24 (18)56 (19)24
(20)32 (21)0 (22)16 (23)8 (24)0 (25)16
(26)16 (27)16 (28)16 (29)16 (30)64 (31)56
(32)8 (33)0 (34)64 (35)0 (36)16 (37) 8
(38)48 (39)40 (40)8 (41)24 (42)56 (43)56
(44)40 (45)40 (46)56 (47)56 (48)40 (49)64
(50)72 (51)24 (52)24 (53)48 (54)0 (55) 8
(56)24 (57)56 (58)48 (59)56 (60)56

DAY 54
(1)64 (2)56 (3)16 (4)64 (5)64 (6)16 (7)5 6
(8)72 (9)40 (10)72 (11)56 (12)64 (13)24
(14)72 (15)72 (16)64 (17)56 (18)48 (19)56
(20)32 (21)56 (22)72 (23)48 (24)32 (25)24
(26)64 (27)48 (28)64 (29)16 (30)40 (31)56
(32)16 (33)40 (34)72 (35)24 (36)72 (37)40
(38)32 (39)48 (40)24 (41)24 (42)16 (43)72
(44)16 (45)40 (46)64 (47)24 (48)16 (49)48
(50)56 (51)24 (52)32 (53)24 (54)48 (55)48
(56)72 (57)48 (58)56 (59)32 (60)40

DAY 55
(1)48 (2)64 (3)72 (4)40 (5)48 (6)24 (7)4 0
(8)72 (9)32 (10)48 (11)16 (12)32 (13)3 2
(14)56 (15)32 (16)56 (17)72 (18)64 (19)4 8
(20)56 (21)32 (22)48 (23)56 (24)64 (25)5 6
(26)48 (27)16 (28)32 (29)24 (30)24 (31)5 6
(32)48 (33)64 (34)56 (35)72 (36)64 (37)4 0
(38)56 (39)32 (40)40 (41)56 (42)56 (43)1 6
(44)72 (45)24 (46)32 (47)72 (48)32 (49)3 2
(50)72 (51)24 (52)48 (53)56 (54)72 (55)7 2
(56)32 (57)48 (58)24 (59)48 (60)56

DAY 56
(1)64 (2)88 (3)16 (4)8 (5)56 (6)32 (7)8
(8)48 (9)8 (10)72 (11)80 (12)40 (13)4 0
(14)88 (15)64 (16)8 (17)32 (18)24 (19)80
(20)32 (21)48 (22)32 (23)72 (24)24 (25)48
(26)96 (27)32 (28)88 (29)32 (30)80 (31)16
(32)80 (33)40 (34)56 (35)80 (36)72 (37)96
(38)56 (39)24 (40)0 (41)80 (42)64 (43)48
(44)80 (45)24 (46)16 (47)80 (48)88 (49)96
(50)80 (51)96 (52)72 (53)80 (54)80 (55)72
(56)8 (57)80 (58)72 (59)0 (60)0

DAY 57
(1)40 (2)40 (3)64 (4)80 (5)96 (6)64 (7)8 0
(8)24 (9)56 (10)24 (11)16 (12)56 (13)24
(14)96 (15)24 (16)32 (17)80 (18)48 (19)1 6
(20)40 (21)72 (22)24 (23)48 (24)72 (25)4 0
(26)88 (27)48 (28)24 (29)88 (30)24 (31)9 6
(32)96 (33)64 (34)32 (35)64 (36)32 (37)8 8
(38)40 (39)32 (40)24 (41)32 (42)96 (43)80
(44)32 (45)64 (46)72 (47)56 (48)64 (49)64
(50)40 (51)64 (52)56 (53)96 (54)40 (55)24
(56)24 (57)32 (58)40 (59)88 (60)80

DAY 58
(1)48 (2)56 (3)32 (4)48 (5)40 (6)56 (7)8 0
(8)56 (9)32 (10)16 (11)72 (12)56 (13)32
(14)16 (15)48 (16)80 (17)56 (18)32 (19)96
(20)96 (21)96 (22)56 (23)72 (24)72 (25)88
(26)32 (27)72 (28)96 (29)56 (30)72 (31)48
(32)32 (33)24 (34)64 (35)64 (36)64 (37)72
(38)48 (39)88 (40)32 (41)64 (42)16 (43)32
(44)48 (45)24 (46)24 (47)56 (48)72 (49)32
(50)48 (51)48 (52)32 (53)24 (54)16 (55)96
(56)56 (57)24 (58)80 (59)72 (60)48

DAY 59
(1)88 (2)88 (3)72 (4)16 (5)64 (6)80 (7)9 6
(8)80 (9)88 (10)88 (11)16 (12)96 (13)96
(14)48 (15)80 (16)32 (17)32 (18)24 (19)88
(20)24 (21)32 (22)56 (23)80 (24)72 (25)72
(26)16 (27)80 (28)32 (29)16 (30)48 (31)72
(32)80 (33)64 (34)80 (35)80 (36)48 (37)72
(38)64 (39)88 (40)72 (41)72 (42)32 (43)96
(44)16 (45)96 (46)24 (47)32 (48)16 (49)56
(50)56 (51)88 (52)16 (53)96 (54)88 (55)40
(56)56 (57)64 (58)56 (59)56 (60)96

DAY 60
(1)63 (2)81 (3)72 (4)36 (5)27 (6)18 (7)6 3
(8)54 (9)63 (10)27 (11)18 (12)72 (13)6 3
(14)45 (15)81 (16)63 (17)72 (18)81 (19)5 4
(20)45 (21)72 (22)27 (23)54 (24)81 (25)4 5
(26)18 (27)27 (28)18 (29)54 (30)45 (31)4 5
(32)81 (33)63 (34)81 (35)36 (36)45 (37)1 8
(38)36 (39)45 (40)27 (41)18 (42)81 (43)5 4
(44)36 (45)27 (46)81 (47)63 (48)54 (49)1 8
(50)36 (51)18 (52)36 (53)72 (54)54 (55)54
(56)18 (57)36 (58)18 (59)36 (60)63

ANSWER KEY 🐾

DAY 61
(1)54 (2)36 (3)9 (4)54 (5)18 (6)18 (7)18 (8)63 (9)27 (10)0 (11)54 (12)72 (13)45 (14)0 (15)81 (16)63 (17)18 (18)27 (19)6 3 (20)45 (21)36 (22)81 (23)9 (24)81 (25)2 7 (26)9 (27)36 (28)0 (29)36 (30)54 (31)7 2 (32)27 (33)36 (34)27 (35)18 (36)63 (37)1 8 (38)54 (39)54 (40)54 (41)36 (42)27 (43)9 (44)36 (45)18 (46)27 (47)18 (48)27 (49)1 8 (50)9 (51)45 (52)63 (53)54 (54)45 (55)3 6 (56)27 (57)27 (58)18 (59)81 (60)27

DAY 62
(1)45 (2)54 (3)36 (4)36 (5)63 (6)72 (7)2 7 (8)45 (9)63 (10)36 (11)18 (12)72 (13)3 6 (14)63 (15)72 (16)72 (17)81 (18)27 (19)27 (20)54 (21)63 (22)27 (23)63 (24)18 (25)45 (26)63 (27)72 (28)54 (29)81 (30)45 (31)81 (32)54 (33)27 (34)45 (35)72 (36)63 (37)63 (38)45 (39)18 (40)27 (41)63 (42)63 (43)18 (44)27 (45)63 (46)63 (47)18 (48)36 (49)54 (50)27 (51)27 (52)54 (53)63 (54)72 (55)27 (56)45 (57)27 (58)63 (59)45 (60)63

DAY 63
(1)18 (2)63 (3)36 (4)36 (5)36 (6)63 (7)4 5 (8)45 (9)81 (10)36 (11)45 (12)27 (13)27 (14)27 (15)63 (16)72 (17)54 (18)18 (19)72 (20)81 (21)54 (22)45 (23)18 (24)27 (25)45 (26)36 (27)54 (28)81 (29)18 (30)54 (31)27 (32)54 (33)63 (34)36 (35)18 (36)27 (37)45 (38)18 (39)54 (40)27 (41)54 (42)72 (43)45 (44)45 (45)36 (46)81 (47)72 (48)18 (49)27 (50)27 (51)45 (52)63 (53)45 (54)27 (55)54 (56)27 (57)18 (58)72 (59)81 (60)45

DAY 64
(1)36 (2)81 (3)90 (4)36 (5)108 (6)72 (7)7 2 (8)72 (9)72 (10)72 (11)81 (12)18 (13)99 (14)18 (15)90 (16)18 (17)108 (18)90 (19)90 (20)108 (21)45 (22)108 (23)3 6 (24)99 (25)45 (26)81 (27)54 (28)54 (29)45 (30)18 (31)18 (32)108 (33)45 (34)54 (35)81 (36)90 (37)72 (38)63 (39)108 (40)18 (41)90 (42)99 (43)90 (44)72 (45)90 (46)45 (47)18 (48)72 (49)90 (50)18 (51)54 (52)45 (53)36 (54)99 (55)72 (56)99 (57)90 (58)72 (59)72 (60)45

DAY 65
(1)72 (2)72 (3)36 (4)18 (5)99 (6)90 (7)27 (8)45 (9)27 (10)99 (11)45 (12)27 (13)45 (14)45 (15)81 (16)45 (17)90 (18)36 (19)108 (20)18 (21)54 (22)63 (23)99 (24)81 (25)72 (26)63 (27)36 (28)72 (29)27 (30)63 (31)99 (32)108 (33)27 (34)27 (35)45 (36)108 (37)99 (38)108 (39)99 (40)108 (41)36 (42)108 (43)63 (44)36 (45)18 (46)27 (47)90 (48)45 (49)99 (50)36 (51)72 (52)45 (53)108 (54)54 (55)99 (56)99 (57)108 (58)99 (59)36 (60)72

DAY 66
(1)18 (2)72 (3)36 (4)72 (5)63 (6)18 (7)9 0 (8)90 (9)108 (10)108 (11)81 (12)36 (13) 0 (14)27 (15)63 (16)36 (17)54 (18)90 (19)27 (20)27 (21)90 (22)108 (23)108 (24)27 (25)36 (26)54 (27)36 (28)27 (29)63 (30)36 (31)0 (32)0 (33)99 (34)72 (35)99 (36)9 9 (37)108 (38)27 (39)27 (40)36 (41)72 (42)36 (43)18 (44)36 (45)54 (46)81 (47)54 (48)81 (49)18 (50)36 (51)108 (52)0 (53)45 (54)9 (55)63 (56)99 (57)63 (58)54 (59)54 (60)0

DAY 67
(1)63 (2)72 (3)81 (4)27 (5)54 (6)18 (7)2 7 (8)81 (9)54 (10)45 (11)45 (12)54 (13)8 1 (14)45 (15)54 (16)45 (17)81 (18)36 (19)108 (20)27 (21)81 (22)27 (23)45 (24)27 (25)54 (26)45 (27)99 (28)63 (29)81 (30)81 (31)36 (32)54 (33)27 (34)36 (35)18 (36)18 (37)36 (38)54 (39)45 (40)81 (41)27 (42)99 (43)18 (44)45 (45)99 (46)54 (47)81 (48)63 (49)108 (50)45 (51)45 (52)45 (53)18 (54)63 (55)108 (56)72 (57)63 (58)54 (59)81 (60)45

DAY 68
(1)70 (2)50 (3)80 (4)70 (5)50 (6)80 (7)80 (8)90 (9)80 (10)60 (11)30 (12)30 (13)60 (14)40 (15)70 (16)90 (17)30 (18)90 (19)80 (20)90 (21)60 (22)30 (23)50 (24)60 (25)60 (26)60 (27)60 (28)20 (29)20 (30)80 (31)70 (32)30 (33)30 (34)70 (35)40 (36)80 (37)40 (38)80 (39)60 (40)60 (41)40 (42)40 (43)70 (44)30 (45)30 (46)90 (47)50 (48)60 (49)20 (50)90 (51)20 (52)30 (53)30 (54)80 (55)50 (56)90 (57)90 (58)30 (59)30 (60)60

DAY 69
(1)40 (2)90 (3)50 (4)30 (5)30 (6)50 (7)30 (8)30 (9)30 (10)40 (11)50 (12)80 (13)60 (14)90 (15)20 (16)20 (17)40 (18)20 (19)80 (20)80 (21)80 (22)60 (23)60 (24)60 (25)60 (26)60 (27)40 (28)70 (29)60 (30)30 (31)50 (32)70 (33)50 (34)70 (35)40 (36)30 (37)40 (38)80 (39)30 (40)50 (41)90 (42)40 (43)40 (44)70 (45)60 (46)60 (47)30 (48)50 (49)30 (50)30 (51)30 (52)40 (53)70 (54)70 (55)50 (56)80 (57)90 (58)50 (59)30 (60)60

DAY 70
(1)60 (2)90 (3)30 (4)60 (5)60 (6)50 (7)10 (8)100 (9)70 (10)70 (11)80 (12)70 (13)120 (14)120 (15)60 (16)100 (17)80 (18)80 (19)10 (20)120 (21)120 (22)30 (23)90 (24)90 (25)70 (26)100 (27)20 (28)20 (29)70 (30)30 (31)20 (32)50 (33)40 (34)110 (35)10 (36)50 (37)120 (38)80 (39)20 (40)40 (41)80 (42)10 (43)100 (44)90 (45)80 (46)120 (47)10 (48)40 (49)40 (50)60 (51)110 (52)80 (53)80 (54)100 (55)100 (56)60 (57)120 (58)60 (59)50 (60)30

DAY 71
(1)40 (2)50 (3)90 (4)40 (5)20 (6)80 (7)20 (8)70 (9)100 (10)120 (11)50 (12)20 (13)120 (14)100 (15)80 (16)120 (17)120 (18)40 (19)70 (20)110 (21)60 (22)50 (23)40 (24)60 (25)50 (26)20 (27)30 (28)120 (29)110 (30)20 (31)90 (32)80 (33)90 (34)20 (35)80 (36)50 (37)50 (38)30 (39)110 (40)100 (41)30 (42)30 (43)60 (44)110 (45)120 (46)30 (47)120 (48)20 (49)90 (50)120 (51)110 (52)110 (53)70 (54)40 (55)80 (56)100 (57)30 (58)80 (59)120 (60)70

DAY 72
(1)55 (2)22 (3)33 (4)33 (5)66 (6)33 (7)22 (8)77 (9)22 (10)99 (11)22 (12)22 (13)55 (14)99 (15)44 (16)99 (17)55 (18)22 (19)66 (20)22 (21)33 (22)99 (23)22 (24)55 (25)77 (26)44 (27)44 (28)33 (29)88 (30)33 (31)99 (32)88 (33)77 (34)33 (35)33 (36)66 (37)55 (38)66 (39)33 (40)55 (41)77 (42)33 (43)66 (44)55 (45)55 (46)33 (47)55 (48)99 (49)33 (50)22 (51)88 (52)66 (53)88 (54)44 (55)66 (56)22 (57)44 (58)88 (59)88 (60)22

ANSWER KEY 🐾

DAY 73
(1)44 (2)88 (3)99 (4)44 (5)99 (6)44 (7)66 (8)99 (9)88 (10)88 (11)55 (12)66 (13)88 (14)55 (15)88 (16)77 (17)77 (18)66 (19)77 (20)77 (21)66 (22)77 (23)33 (24)33 (25)88 (26)55 (27)44 (28)55 (29)66 (30)66 (31)44 (32)44 (33)44 (34)66 (35)99 (36)55 (37)55 (38)44 (39)33 (40)33 (41)55 (42)88 (43)22 (44)33 (45)33 (46)99 (47)88 (48)88 (49)99 (50)88 (51)22 (52)88 (53)88 (54)88 (55)66 (56)22 (57)22 (58)99 (59)66 (60)99

DAY 74
(1)66 (2)99 (3)88 (4)11 (5)132 (6)11 (7)44 (8)77 (9)99 (10)99 (11)110 (12)77 (13)99 (14)110 (15)33 (16)121 (17)88 (18)55 (19)66 (20)44 (21)99 (22)55 (23)121 (24)121 (25)88 (26)132 (27)99 (28)77 (29)110 (30)55 (31)22 (32)33 (33)7 7 (34)77 (35)11 (36)99 (37)33 (38)9 9 (39)132 (40)110 (41)132 (42)33 (43)0 (44)121 (45)11 (46)11 (47)121 (48)44 (49)44 (50)121 (51)66 (52)44 (53)121 (54)44 (55)11 (56)121 (57)121 (58)33 (59)11 (60)121

DAY 75
(1)132 (2)22 (3)77 (4)88 (5)110 (6)77 (7)121 (8)132 (9)88 (10)121 (11)44 (12)77 (13)33 (14)88 (15)44 (16)55 (17)33 (18)22 (19)121 (20)121 (21)132 (22)77 (23)88 (24)22 (25)22 (26)121 (27)88 (28)99 (29)77 (30)99 (31)66 (32)121 (33)66 (34)88 (35)33 (36)44 (37)44 (38)55 (39)77 (40)33 (41)66 (42)55 (43)77 (44)22 (45)88 (46)110 (47)121 (48)121 (49)55 (50)55 (51)132 (52)66 (53)110 (54)121 (55)88 (56)110 (57)132 (58)33 (59)110 (60)88

DAY 76
(1)0 (2)96 (3)60 (4)48 (5)84 (6)96 (7)60 (8)60 (9)96 (10)108 (11)0 (12)48 (13)84 (14)48 (15)24 (16)84 (17)12 (18)0 (19)96 (20)48 (21)96 (22)12 (23)60 (24)84 (25)72 (26)36 (27)60 (28)72 (29)60 (30)24 (31)96 (32)36 (33)60 (34)84 (35)96 (36)36 (37)48 (38)72 (39)24 (40)0 (41)24 (42)108 (43)24 (44)84 (45)24 (46)60 (47)72 (48)108 (49)60 (50)12 (51)12 (52)72 (53)48 (54)48 (55)24 (56)24 (57)48 (58)60 (59)12 (60)12

DAY 77
(1)24 (2)96 (3)108 (4)72 (5)108 (6)60 (7)96 (8)84 (9)108 (10)108 (11)72 (12)60 (13)96 (14)108 (15)48 (16)48 (17)60 (18)96 (19)108 (20)108 (21)72 (22)84 (23)108 (24)48 (25)36 (26)48 (27)24 (28)72 (29)84 (30)24 (31)108 (32)84 (33)48 (34)72 (35)96 (36)96 (37)84 (38)36 (39)60 (40)108 (41)96 (42)108 (43)72 (44)36 (45)24 (46)72 (47)24 (48)108 (49)108 (50)108 (51)48 (52)24 (53)108 (54)60 (55)84 (56)72 (57)48 (58)108 (59)36 (60)72

DAY 78
(1)84 (2)72 (3)84 (4)108 (5)36 (6)84 (7)108 (8)84 (9)72 (10)24 (11)48 (12)108 (13)72 (14)24 (15)72 (16)108 (17)84 (18)108 (19)84 (20)48 (21)60 (22)48 (23)96 (24)36 (25)96 (26)24 (27)108 (28)60 (29)108 (30)36 (31)60 (32)36 (33)72 (34)60 (35)24 (36)60 (37)36 (38)72 (39)48 (40)84 (41)48 (42)108 (43)36 (44)72 (45)108 (46)72 (47)108 (48)48 (49)48 (50)24 (51)36 (52)72 (53)96 (54)48 (55)36 (56)96 (57)24 (58)24 (59)84 (60)48

DAY 79
(1)108 (2)36 (3)24 (4)84 (5)108 (6)108 (7)96 (8)96 (9)60 (10)108 (11)108 (12)60 (13)24 (14)96 (15)24 (16)60 (17)84 (18)84 (19)48 (20)108 (21)96 (22)84 (23)96 (24)108 (25)96 (26)96 (27)84 (28)72 (29)108 (30)60 (31)60 (32)96 (33)108 (34)60 (35)48 (36)84 (37)108 (38)96 (39)36 (40)60 (41)108 (42)84 (43)24 (44)96 (45)60 (46)72 (47)96 (48)24 (49)108 (50)24 (51)48 (52)96 (53)96 (54)84 (55)72 (56)72 (57)108 (58)108 (59)36 (60)72

DAY 80
(1)120 (2)108 (3)36 (4)72 (5)132 (6)108 (7)60 (8)96 (9)84 (10)120 (11)36 (12)60 (13)120 (14)36 (15)72 (16)36 (17)60 (18)72 (19)48 (20)36 (21)72 (22)120 (23)132 (24)84 (25)48 (26)84 (27)36 (28)60 (29)24 (30)48 (31)60 (32)120 (33)108 (34)48 (35)120 (36)108 (37)36 (38)36 (39)24 (40)36 (41)132 (42)24 (43)48 (44)24 (45)24 (46)108 (47)72 (48)108 (49)132 (50)48 (51)84 (52)96 (53)48 (54)60 (55)96 (56)72 (57)24 (58)84 (59)48 (60)120

DAY 81
(1)144 (2)84 (3)36 (4)0 (5)60 (6)144 (7)48 (8)84 (9)72 (10)120 (11)12 (12)72 (13)60 (14)12 (15)60 (16)60 (17)96 (18)12 (19)48 (20)72 (21)0 (22)120 (23)60 (24)48 (25)96 (26)144 (27)12 (28)0 (29)132 (30)132 (31)72 (32)24 (33)60 (34)132 (35)108 (36)12 (37)24 (38)24 (39)36 (40)120 (41)60 (42)132 (43)36 (44)36 (45)108 (46)36 (47)144 (48)36 (49)84 (50)60 (51)12 (52)0 (53)24 (54)0 (55)12 (56)72 (57)132 (58)12 (59)120 (60)96

DAY 82
(1)132 (2)48 (3)144 (4)132 (5)24 (6)96 (7)132 (8)120 (9)48 (10)84 (11)132 (12)60 (13)84 (14)96 (15)84 (16)60 (17)60 (18)120 (19)72 (20)72 (21)96 (22)48 (23)96 (24)132 (25)60 (26)132 (27)72 (28)120 (29)144 (30)24 (31)84 (32)36 (33)132 (34)144 (35)120 (36)120 (37)108 (38)72 (39)96 (40)96 (41)144 (42)84 (43)108 (44)120 (45)60 (46)36 (47)108 (48)120 (49)60 (50)96 (51)144 (52)144 (53)96 (54)108 (55)72 (56)108 (57)132 (58)60 (59)60 (60)96

DAY 83
(1)84 (2)108 (3)108 (4)48 (5)96 (6)60 (7)36 (8)72 (9)24 (10)48 (11)48 (12)84 (13)144 (14)96 (15)108 (16)108 (17)24 (18)144 (19)120 (20)120 (21)144 (22)24 (23)36 (24)24 (25)72 (26)60 (27)84 (28)72 (29)144 (30)24 (31)144 (32)108 (33)108 (34)132 (35)144 (36)48 (37)48 (38)84 (39)36 (40)24 (41)132 (42)48 (43)84 (44)96 (45)96 (46)60 (47)48 (48)120 (49)48 (50)144 (51)72 (52)96 (53)48 (54)60 (55)144 (56)48 (57)84 (58)84 (59)84 (60)96

DAY 84
(1)12 (2)60 (3)6 (4)40 (5)8 (6)90 (7)66 (8)50 (9)45 (10)70 (11)36 (12)144 (13)56 (14)70 (15)55 (16)72 (17)84 (18)30 (19)50 (20)55 (21)8 (22)84 (23)12 (24)18 (25)80 (26)60 (27)77 (28)30 (29)77 (30)55 (31)12 (32)33 (33)28 (34)64 (35)16 (36)32 (37)14 (38)49 (39)55 (40)54 (41)24 (42)88 (43)49 (44)16 (45)50 (46)54 (47)120 (48)48 (49)48 (50)63 (51)50 (52)12 (53)18 (54)44 (55)60 (56)16 (57)144 (58)84 (59)110 (60)72

ANSWER KEY 🐾

DAY 85
(1)33 (2)28 (3)72 (4)24 (5)30 (6)36 (7)88
(8)8 (9)24 (10)24 (11)60 (12)22 (13)12
(14)9 (15)72 (16)96 (17)14 (18)25 (19)32
(20)32 (21)121 (22)60 (23)20 (24)54
(25)20 (26)21 (27)84 (28)110 (29)84
(30)55 (31)54 (32)24 (33)22 (34)18
(35)100 (36)120 (37)6 (38)8 (39)36 (40)84
(41)60 (42)40 (43)21 (44)40 (45)36 (46)18
(47)10 (48)70 (49)18 (50)110 (51)24
(52)99 (53)90 (54)108 (55)84 (56)16
(57)90 (58)16 (59)8 (60)27

DAY 86
(1)132 (2)55 (3)66 (4)77 (5)99 (6)88 (7)84
(8)32 (9)15 (10)64 (11)16 (12)72 (13)30
(14)44 (15)16 (16)60 (17)22 (18)63
(19)120 (20)77 (21)60 (22)36 (23)66
(24)42 (25)66 (26)22 (27)110 (28)24
(29)40 (30)35 (31)40 (32)28 (33)16
(34)108 (35)60 (36)36 (37)45 (38)32
(39)49 (40)25 (41)24 (42)99 (43)20 (44)96
(45)48 (46)33 (47)63 (48)121 (49)40
(50)16 (51)56 (52)12 (53)6 (54)66 (55)54
(56)6 (57)100 (58)27 (59)48 (60)60

DAY 87
(1)48 (2)24 (3)90 (4)22 (5)14 (6)99 (7)24
(8)56 (9)72 (10)63 (11)100 (12)45 (13)28
(14)121 (15)44 (16)14 (17)36 (18)18
(19)12 (20)21 (21)55 (22)12 (23)66 (24)4
(25)12 (26)55 (27)25 (28)77 (29)144
(30)77 (31)24 (32)30 (33)44 (34)15 (35)18
(36)72 (37)90 (38)14 (39)72 (40)36 (41)56
(42)54 (43)22 (44)36 (45)42 (46)50 (47)16
(48)35 (49)132 (50)44 (51)45 (52)40
(53)20 (54)77 (55)36 (56)16 (57)88 (58)72
(59)32 (60)110

DAY 88
(1)77 (2)24 (3)0 (4)16 (5)7 (6)24 (7)40
(8)36 (9)48 (10)108 (11)55 (12)0 (13)8
(14)40 (15)24 (16)5 (17)15 (18)30 (19)70
(20)72 (21)0 (22)36 (23)99 (24)12 (25)24
(26)20 (27)20 (28)36 (29)120 (30)0 (31)0
(32)36 (33)28 (34)28 (35)24 (36)28 (37)36
(38)36 (39)36 (40)0 (41)10 (42)9 (43)108
(44)88 (45)0 (46)7 (47)40 (48)36 (49)22
(50)32 (51)144 (52)144 (53)56 (54)70
(55)15 (56)0 (57)30 (58)48 (59)49 (60)16

DAY 89
(1)80 (2)12 (3)30 (4)12 (5)63 (6)56 (7)42
(8)48 (9)15 (10)108 (11)8 (12)16 (13)144
(14)132 (15)24 (16)110 (17)40 (18)15
(19)35 (20)84 (21)32 (22)22 (23)36 (24)12
(25)63 (26)36 (27)24 (28)12 (29)22 (30)80
(31)12 (32)8 (33)48 (34)12 (35)35 (36)10
(37)24 (38)72 (39)14 (40)30 (41)36 (42)42
(43)20 (44)70 (45)24 (46)16 (47)40 (48)16
(49)18 (50)24 (51)35 (52)8 (53)24 (54)32
(55)48 (56)72 (57)4 (58)99 (59)44 (60)44

DAY 90
(1)99 (2)18 (3)110 (4)16 (5)30 (6)84 (7)28
(8)22 (9)72 (10)12 (11)50 (12)66 (13)24
(14)30 (15)100 (16)84 (17)40 (18)16 (19)6
(20)132 (21)48 (22)40 (23)24 (24)81
(25)120 (26)120 (27)24 (28)132 (29)8
(30)96 (31)50 (32)35 (33)90 (34)12 (35)14
(36)18 (37)12 (38)18 (39)30 (40)12 (41)55
(42)84 (43)99 (44)36 (45)63 (46)50 (47)35
(48)42 (49)50 (50)15 (51)121 (52)42
(53)12 (54)110 (55)45 (56)32 (57)84
(58)24 (59)88 (60)20

DAY 91
(1)36 (2)40 (3)60 (4)50 (5)90 (6)84 (7)22
(8)35 (9)120 (10)10 (11)144 (12)8 (13)36
(14)27 (15)132 (16)30 (17)18 (18)99
(19)80 (20)20 (21)48 (22)132 (23)81
(24)40 (25)36 (26)55 (27)90 (28)144
(29)33 (30)50 (31)22 (32)72 (33)44
(34)144 (35)36 (36)55 (37)28 (38)64
(39)15 (40)45 (41)24 (42)22 (43)50 (44)55
(45)12 (46)14 (47)50 (48)8 (49)120 (50)48
(51)32 (52)36 (53)24 (54)88 (55)90 (56)55
(57)21 (58)27 (59)18 (60)60

DAY 92
(1)77 (2)42 (3)50 (4)30 (5)18 (6)90 (7)110
(8)36 (9)60 (10)144 (11)63 (12)63 (13)32
(14)30 (15)84 (16)21 (17)66 (18)40 (19)56
(20)21 (21)90 (22)60 (23)27 (24)50 (25)45
(26)60 (27)18 (28)45 (29)72 (30)60 (31)63
(32)55 (33)30 (34)40 (35)63 (36)36 (37)49
(38)18 (39)28 (40)32 (41)24 (42)36 (43)54
(44)100 (45)35 (46)45 (47)56 (48)77
(49)20 (50)66 (51)32 (52)90 (53)54 (54)88
(55)35 (56)55 (57)24 (58)132 (59)18
(60)60

DAY 93
(1)21 (2)48 (3)18 (4)30 (5)16 (6)40 (7)90
(8)77 (9)96 (10)48 (11)24 (12)55 (13)42
(14)28 (15)27 (16)56 (17)18 (18)18 (19)14
(20)110 (21)36 (22)50 (23)132 (24)63
(25)45 (26)32 (27)14 (28)108 (29)36
(30)80 (31)15 (32)80 (33)18 (34)40 (35)77
(36)35 (37)48 (38)63 (39)32 (40)45 (41)20
(42)4 (43)33 (44)9 (45)10 (46)42 (47)66
(48)48 (49)81 (50)20 (51)42 (52)120
(53)45 (54)6 (55)27 (56)132 (57)72 (58)72
(59)12 (60)27

DAY 94
(1)40 (2)54 (3)90 (4)77 (5)70 (6)80 (7)60
(8)84 (9)18 (10)70 (11)84 (12)88 (13)90
(14)16 (15)99 (16)33 (17)72 (18)12 (19)20
(20)49 (21)20 (22)55 (23)25 (24)66 (25)84
(26)15 (27)72 (28)55 (29)9 (30)84 (31)25
(32)32 (33)42 (34)24 (35)24 (36)36
(37)120 (38)132 (39)25 (40)16 (41)100
(42)24 (43)35 (44)54 (45)121 (46)33
(47)18 (48)108 (49)48 (50)12 (51)144
(52)36 (53)56 (54)96 (55)44 (56)27 (57)28
(58)72 (59)72 (60)96

DAY 95
(1)36 (2)10 (3)144 (4)108 (5)64 (6)9 (7)72
(8)12 (9)32 (10)40 (11)36 (12)48 (13)44
(14)84 (15)20 (16)0 (17)5 (18)18 (19)54
(20)10 (21)80 (22)0 (23)36 (24)40 (25)70
(26)25 (27)24 (28)24 (29)30 (30)66 (31)60
(32)40 (33)48 (34)20 (35)28 (36)90 (37)33
(38)36 (39)48 (40)120 (41)36 (42)32
(43)12 (44)28 (45)36 (46)28 (47)21 (48)0
(49)120 (50)60 (51)12 (52)54 (53)88
(54)55 (55)8 (56)108 (57)66 (58)72 (59)24
(60)80

DAY 96
(1)4 (2)48 (3)28 (4)14 (5)18 (6)88 (7)36
(8)72 (9)24 (10)24 (11)48 (12)70 (13)64
(14)72 (15)72 (16)24 (17)96 (18)36 (19)99
(20)99 (21)21 (22)27 (23)20 (24)32 (25)36
(26)132 (27)27 (28)64 (29)60 (30)35
(31)12 (32)49 (33)40 (34)24 (35)24 (36)66
(37)54 (38)32 (39)90 (40)8 (41)55 (42)132
(43)80 (44)33 (45)21 (46)20 (47)80 (48)72
(49)84 (50)64 (51)24 (52)27 (53)16 (54)77
(55)48 (56)10 (57)10 (58)54 (59)42
(60)132

ANSWER KEY 🐾

DAY 97
(1)99 (2)96 (3)30 (4)33 (5)20 (6)56 (7)15
(8)60 (9)132 (10)15 (11)24 (12)110 (13)24
(14)44 (15)15 (16)35 (17)88 (18)90 (19)96
(20)88 (21)25 (22)36 (23)21 (24)99 (25)44
(26)88 (27)30 (28)70 (29)12 (30)35 (31)12
(32)27 (33)80 (34)132 (35)96 (36)10
(37)18 (38)21 (39)20 (40)72 (41)90 (42)24
(43)16 (44)80 (45)20 (46)60 (47)14 (48)18
(49)81 (50)36 (51)48 (52)70 (53)18 (54)66
(55)30 (56)132 (57)18 (58)35 (59)55
(60)24

DAY 98
(1)42 (2)24 (3)18 (4)18 (5)80 (6)48 (7)144
(8)24 (9)21 (10)4 (11)44 (12)120 (13)45
(14)77 (15)27 (16)4 (17)27 (18)45 (19)20
(20)40 (21)63 (22)21 (23)72 (24)45 (25)72
(26)16 (27)33 (28)16 (29)54 (30)33 (31)28
(32)42 (33)110 (34)70 (35)88 (36)108
(37)80 (38)70 (39)132 (40)55 (41)20
(42)132 (43)144 (44)30 (45)14 (46)24
(47)20 (48)42 (49)56 (50)24 (51)36 (52)18
(53)8 (54)48 (55)24 (56)24 (57)45 (58)20
(59)48 (60)50

DAY 99
(1)77 (2)36 (3)36 (4)42 (5)121 (6)27 (7)20
(8)28 (9)28 (10)33 (11)33 (12)60 (13)8
(14)99 (15)90 (16)60 (17)32 (18)48 (19)84
(20)30 (21)55 (22)54 (23)120 (24)12
(25)25 (26)55 (27)14 (28)18 (29)36 (30)40
(31)16 (32)50 (33)99 (34)84 (35)24 (36)48
(37)28 (38)20 (39)80 (40)77 (41)16 (42)54
(43)66 (44)42 (45)99 (46)28 (47)28 (48)12
(49)35 (50)60 (51)12 (52)48 (53)40 (54)10
(55)27 (56)9 (57)48 (58)80 (59)132 (60)44

DAY 100
(1)30 (2)80 (3)80 (4)45 (5)77 (6)40 (7)60
(8)21 (9)100 (10)40 (11)72 (12)18 (13)55
(14)80 (15)63 (16)24 (17)63 (18)48 (19)70
(20)30 (21)20 (22)48 (23)12 (24)40 (25)4
(26)24 (27)20 (28)14 (29)16 (30)84
(31)108 (32)66 (33)40 (34)80 (35)49
(36)88 (37)27 (38)32 (39)54 (40)50 (41)84
(42)22 (43)60 (44)40 (45)12 (46)44 (47)60
(48)36 (49)45 (50)33 (51)24 (52)120
(53)42 (54)60 (55)48 (56)54 (57)42 (58)24
(59)50 (60)24

www.ingramcontent.com/pod-product-compliance
Lightning Source LLC
Chambersburg PA
CBHW052115020426
42335CB00021B/2771